2ND EDITION

Better Learning

Through Structured Teaching

A Framework
for the
Gradual Release
of Responsibility

Douglas Fisher
Nancy Frey

Alexandria, VA USA

1703 N. Beauregard St. • Alexandria, VA 22311-1714 USA
Phone: 800-933-2723 or 703-578-9600 • Fax: 703-575-5400
Website: www.ascd.org • E-mail: member@ascd.org
Author guidelines: www.ascd.org/write

Gene R. Carter, *Executive Director;* Mary Catherine (MC) Desrosiers, *Chief Program Development Officer;* Richard Papale, *Publisher;* Genny Ostertag, *Acquisitions Editor;* Julie Houtz, *Director, Book Editing & Production;* Katie Martin, *Editor;* Louise Bova, *Senior Graphic Designer;* Mike Kalyan, *Production Manager;* Cindy Stock, *Typesetter;* Kyle Steichen, *Production Specialist*

PAPERBACK ISBN: 978-1-4166-1629-0   ASCD product #113006

ASCD Member Book No. FY14-3 (Dec. 2013, P). ASCD Member Books mail to Premium (P), Select (S), and Institutional Plus (I+) members on this schedule: Jan, PSI+; Feb, P; Apr, PSI+; May, P; Jul, PSI+; Aug, P; Sep, PSI+; Nov, PSI+; Dec, P. For up-to-date details on membership, see www.ascd.org/membership.

Also available as an e-book (see Books in Print for the ISBNs).

Quantity discounts: 10–49 copies, 10%; 50+ copies, 15%; for 1,000 or more copies, call 800-933-2723, ext. 5634, or 703-575-5634. For desk copies: www.ascd.org/deskcopy

Library of Congress Cataloging-in-Publication Data

Fisher, Douglas, 1965–
    Better learning through structured teaching / Douglas Fisher and Nancy Frey. — Second edition.
        pages cm
    Includes bibliographical references and index.
    ISBN 978-1-4166-1629-0 (pbk. : alk. paper) 1. Active learning. 2. Teaching. 3. Constructivism (Education) I. Frey, Nancy, 1959– II. Title.
    LB1027.23.F575 2014
    371.102—dc23
                            2013031423

23 22 21 20 19 18 17 16 15 14   3 4 5 6 7 8 9 10 11 12

Better
Learning
Through Structured Teaching

**A Framework for the
Gradual Release of Responsibility**

Learning, or Not Learning, in School

Learning—the goal of schooling—is a complex process. But what *is* learning? Consider the following definitions and the implications each has for teaching:

- Learning is the process of acquiring knowledge or skill through study, experience, or teaching.
- Learning is experience that brings about a relatively permanent change in behavior.
- Learning is a change in neural function as a consequence of experience.
- Learning is the cognitive process of acquiring skill or knowledge.
- Learning is an increase in the amount of response rules and concepts in the memory of an intelligent system.

Which definition fits with your beliefs? Now ask yourself, how is it that *you* learn? Think of something that you do well. Take a minute to analyze this skill or behavior. How did you develop your prowess? How did you move from novice to expert? You probably did not develop a high level of skill from simply being told how to complete a task. Instead, you likely had models, feedback, peer support, and lots of practice. Over time, you developed your expertise. You may have extended that expertise further by sharing it with others. The model that explains this type of learning process is called *the gradual release of responsibility instructional framework.*

The Gradual Release of Responsibility Instructional Framework

The gradual release of responsibility instructional framework purposefully shifts the cognitive load from teacher-as-model, to joint responsibility of teacher and learner, to independent practice and application by the learner (Pearson & Gallagher, 1983). It stipulates that the teacher moves from assuming "all the responsibility for performing a task . . . to a situation in which the students assume all of the responsibility" (Duke & Pearson, 2002, p. 211). This gradual release may occur over a day, a week, a month, or a year. Graves and Fitzgerald (2003) note that "effective instruction often follows a progression in which teachers gradually do less of the work and students gradually assume increased responsibility for their learning. It is through this process of gradually assuming more and more responsibility for their learning that students become competent, independent learners" (p. 98).

The gradual release of responsibility framework, originally developed for reading instruction, reflects the intersection of several theories, including

- Piaget's (1952) work on cognitive structures and schemata
- Vygotsky's (1962, 1978) work on zones of proximal development
- Bandura's (1965) work on attention, retention, reproduction, and motivation
- Wood, Bruner, and Ross's (1976) work on scaffolded instruction

Taken together, these theories suggest that learning occurs through interactions with others; when these interactions are intentional, specific learning occurs.

Unfortunately, most current efforts to implement the gradual release of responsibility framework limit these interactions to adult and child exchanges: *I do it; we do it together; you do it.* But this three-phase model omits a truly vital component: students learning through collaboration with their peers—the *you do it together* phase. Although the effectiveness of peer learning has been demonstrated with English language learners (Zhang & Dougherty Stahl, 2011), students with disabilities (Grenier, Dyson, & Yeaton, 2005), and learners identified as gifted (Patrick, Bangel, & Jeon, 2005), it has typically been examined as a singular practice, isolated from the overall instructional design of the lesson. A more complete implementation model for the gradual release of responsibility recognizes the recursive nature of learning and has teachers cycle purposefully through purpose setting and guided instruction, collaborative learning, and independent experiences. In Figure 1.1, we map out these phases of learning, indicating the share of responsibility that students and teachers have in each.

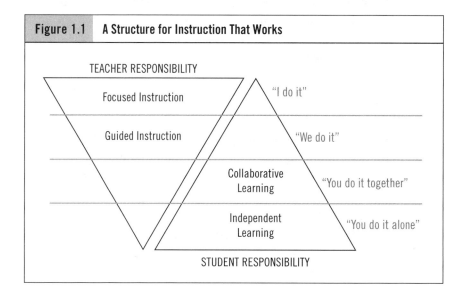

| Figure 1.1 | A Structure for Instruction That Works |

TEACHER RESPONSIBILITY

Focused Instruction — "I do it"

Guided Instruction — "We do it"

Collaborative Learning — "You do it together"

Independent Learning — "You do it alone"

STUDENT RESPONSIBILITY

We are not suggesting that every lesson must always start with focused instruction (goal setting and modeling) before progressing to guided instruction, then to collaborative learning, and finally to independent tasks (Grant, Lapp, Fisher, Johnson, & Frey, 2012). Teachers often reorder the phases—for example, begin a lesson with an independent task, such as bellwork or a quick-write, or engage students in collaborative peer inquiry prior to providing teacher modeling. As we stress throughout this book, what is important and necessary for deep learning is that students experience all four phases of learning when encountering new content. We will explore these phases in greater detail in subsequent chapters, but let's proceed now with an overview of each.

Focused Instruction

Focused instruction is an important part of the overall lesson design. This phase includes establishing a clear lesson purpose. We use the word *purpose* rather than *goal, objective,* or *learning target* because it's essential to ensure that students grasp the relevance of the lesson. The statement of a lesson's purpose can address goals related to content, language, and social aspects. Consider, for example, the teacher who clearly communicates the purpose of a lesson as follows:

> Our content goal today is to multiply and estimate products of fractions and mixed numerals because these are used in cooking, construction, and medicine. Our language goal for today is to use precise mathematical terminology while discussing problems and answers with one another. Our social goal today is to improve our turn-taking skills by making sure that each member of the group has a chance to participate in the discussion.

As Dick, Carey, and Carey (2001) remind us, an "instructional goal is (1) a clear, general statement of learner outcomes,

(2) related to an identified problem and needs assessment, and (3) achievable through instruction" (p. 25). These are important considerations when establishing lesson purpose. As we will discuss further in Chapter 2, it's not enough to simply state the lesson purpose. We must ensure that students have opportunities to engage with the purpose in a meaningful way and obtain feedback about their performance.

In addition to establishing purpose, the focused instruction phase of learning provides students with information about the ways in which a skilled reader, writer, or thinker processes the information under discussion. Typically, this is done through direct explanations, modeling, or think-alouds in which the teacher demonstrates the kind of thinking required to solve a problem, understand a set of directions, or interact with a text. For example, after reading aloud a passage about spiders to 3rd graders, a teacher might say:

> Now I have even more questions. I just read that spiders don't have mouth parts, so I'm wondering how they eat. I can't really visualize that, and I will definitely have to look for more information to answer that question. I didn't know that spiders are found all over the world—that was interesting to find out. To me, the most interesting spider mentioned in this text is the one that lives underwater in silken domes. Now, that is something I need to know more about.

Focused instruction is typically done with the whole class and usually lasts 15 minutes or less—long enough to clearly establish purpose and ensure that students have a model from which to work. Note that focused instruction does not have to come at the beginning of the lesson, nor is there any reason to limit focused instruction to once per lesson. The gradual release of responsibility instructional framework is recursive, and a teacher might reassume responsibility several times during a lesson to reestablish its purpose and provide additional examples of expert thinking.

Guided Instruction

The guided instruction phase of a lesson is almost always conducted with small, purposeful groups that have been composed based on formative assessment data. There are a number of instructional routines that can be used during guided instruction, and we will explore these further in Chapter 3. The key to effective guided instruction is planning. These are not random groups of students meeting with the teacher; the groups consist of students who share a common instructional need that the teacher can address.

Guided instruction is an ideal time to differentiate. As Tomlinson and Imbeau (2010) have noted, teachers can differentiate content, process, and product. Small-group instruction allows teachers to vary the instructional materials they use, the level of prompting or questioning they employ, and the products they expect. For example, Marcus Moore,* a 7th grade science teacher, identified a group of five students who did not perform well on a subset of pre-assessment questions related to asteroid impacts. He met with this group of students and shared with them a short book from the school library called *Comets, Asteroids, and Meteorites* (Gallant, 2000). He asked each student to read specific pages related to asteroids and then to participate in a discussion with him and the others in the group about the potential effect that these bodies might have on Earth. During this 20-minute lesson, Mr. Moore validated and extended his students' understanding that, throughout history, life on Earth has been disrupted by major catastrophic events, including asteroids. At one point in the group's discussion, he provided this prompt:

---

*All the teachers and students we discuss in this book are real people, with names changed to protect their privacy.

> Consider what you know about the Earth's surface. Talk about that—is it all flat? *(Students all respond no.)* What do you think are the things that made the surface of the Earth look like it does? Remember, the Earth has a history. . . .

A single guided instructional event won't translate into all students developing the content knowledge or skills they are lacking, but a series of guided instructional events will. Over time and with cues, prompts, and questions, teachers can guide students to increasingly complex thinking. Guided instruction is, in part, about establishing high expectations and providing the support so that students can reach those expectations.

Collaborative Learning

As we have noted, the collaborative learning phase of instruction is too often neglected. If used at all, it tends to be a special event rather than an established instructional routine. When done right, collaborative learning is a way for students to consolidate their thinking and understanding. Negotiating with peers, discussing ideas and information, and engaging in inquiry with others gives students the opportunity to use what they have learned during focused and guided instruction.

Collaborative learning is not the time to introduce new information to students. This phase of instruction is a time for students to apply what they already know in novel situations or engage in a spiral review of previous knowledge.

It is important, too, that you allow collaborative learning to be a little experimental, a little messy. In order for students to consolidate their thinking and interact meaningfully with the content and one another, they need to encounter tasks that will reveal their partial understandings and misconceptions as well as confirm what they already know. In other words, wrestling with a problem is a necessary condition of collaborative learning. If you are pretty certain your students will be able to complete a collaborative learning task accurately the first time through, that task would probably be better suited to the independent learning phase.

Collaborative learning is also a perfect opportunity for students to engage in accountable talk and argumentation. *Accountable talk* is a framework for teaching students about discourse in order to enrich these interactions. First developed by Lauren Resnick (2000) and a team of researchers at the Institute for Learning at the University of Pittsburgh, accountable talk describes the agreements students and their teacher commit to as they engage in partner conversations. These include staying on topic, using information that is accurate and appropriate for the topic, and thinking deeply about what the partner has to say. Students are taught to be accountable for the content and to one another, and they learn techniques for keeping the conversation moving forward, toward a richer understanding of the topic at hand. The Institute for Learning (n.d.) describes five indicators of accountable talk:

1. Press for clarification and explanation (e.g., "Could you describe what you mean?").
2. Require justification of proposals and challenges (e.g., "Where did you find that information?").
3. Recognize and challenge misconception (e.g., "I don't agree, because _____.").
4. Demand evidence for claims and arguments (e.g., "Can you give me an example?").
5. Interpret and use one another's statements (e.g., "I think David's saying _____, in which case, maybe we should _____.").

These are important skills for students to master and, on a larger scale, valuable tools for all citizens in a participatory democracy (Michaels, O'Connor, & Resnick, 2008). They are also key to meeting Common Core State Standards in speaking and listening, the first of which asks students to "prepare for and participate effectively in a range of conversations and collaborations with diverse partners, building on others' ideas and expressing their own clearly and persuasively" (National Governors Association Center for Best Practices, Council of Chief State School Officers [NGA/CCSSO], 2010a, p. 22).

We have seen teachers integrate collaborative learning opportunities into their instruction in a variety of ways. For example, a 10th grade social studies teacher selected a number of readings that would allow his students to compare and contrast the Glorious Revolution of England, the American Revolution, and the French Revolution. The students did so through reciprocal teaching (Palinscar & Brown, 1984), an arrangement in which groups of students read a piece of text in common; discuss the text using predicting, questioning, summarizing, and clarifying; and take notes on their discussion. At the end of the discussion, each student in the class summarizes the reading individually—a step that ensures the individual accountability that is key to successful collaborative learning.

The way in which one of these groups of students talked about their reading demonstrates how peers can support one another in the consolidation of information:

> *Jamal:* I still don't get it. Those folks in England had a revolution because the king wanted the army to be Catholic, and he got his own friends in government. But I need help to clarify what they mean by the "Dispensing Power." It sounds all Harry Potter.
>
> *Antone:* I feel you. But dispensing power—that's just the name for getting rid of rules you don't want.
>
> *LaSheika:* That king, James number 2, used a power he had to suspend laws and other rules. Adding that to the things you

said already, it made people very angry, and they started the revolution to get rid of him. It's just like the other revolutions we talked about.

Collaborative learning situations help students think through key ideas, are a natural opportunity for inquiry, and promote engagement with the content. As such, they are critical to the successful implementation of the gradual release of responsibility instructional framework.

Independent Learning

The ultimate goal of instruction is that students be able to independently apply information, ideas, content, skills, and strategies in unique situations. We want to create learners who are not dependent on others for information and ideas. As such, students need practice completing independent tasks and learning from those tasks. Overall and across time, the school and instructional events must be "organized to encourage and support a continued, increasingly mature and comprehensive acceptance of responsibilities for one's own learning" (Kesten, 1987, p. 15). The effectiveness of independent learning, however, depends on students' readiness to engage in it; too many students are asked to complete independent tasks without having received the focused or guided instruction they need.

When students are ready to apply skills and knowledge to produce new products, there is a range of independent tasks that might be used. Our experience suggests that the more authentic a task is, the more likely the student is to complete it. For example, a kindergarten teacher might ask a student to read a familiar book to three adults, a 6th grade science teacher might ask a student to predict the outcome of a lab based on the previous three experiments, and a high school art teacher might ask a student to incorporate light and perspective into a new painting. What's essential is that an independent learning task clearly relate to the instruction each student has received and yet also provide the student an opportunity to apply the resulting knowledge in a new way.

When Learning Isn't Occurring

With this structure for instruction that works fresh in mind, let's look at some structures that don't work so well. Unfortunately, there are still plenty of classrooms in which responsibility for learning is *not* being transferred from knowledgeable others (teachers, peers, parents) to students. Although they may feature some of the phases of instruction we have described, the omission of other phases derails learning in significant ways.

For example, in some classrooms, teachers provide modeling and then skip straight to asking students to complete independent tasks—an approach graphically represented in Figure 1.2.

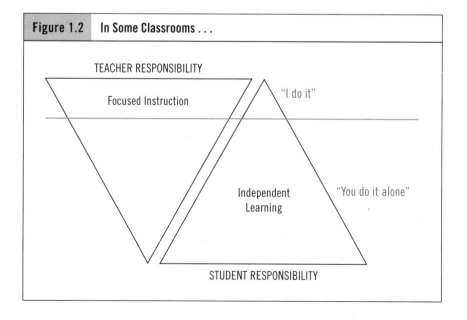

| Figure 1.2 | In Some Classrooms . . . |

TEACHER RESPONSIBILITY

Focused Instruction

"I do it"

Independent Learning

"You do it alone"

STUDENT RESPONSIBILITY

This instructional model is very familiar. A teacher demonstrates how to solve algebra problems and then asks students to solve the odd-numbered problems in the back of the book. A teacher reads a text aloud and then asks students to complete a comprehension worksheet based on the reading. In both cases, the teacher fails to develop students' understanding of the content through the purposeful interaction of guided instruction.

Sadly, there is a classroom model even worse than this, at least in terms of instructional development. It's the one in which students are asked to learn everything on their own, depicted in Figure 1.3.

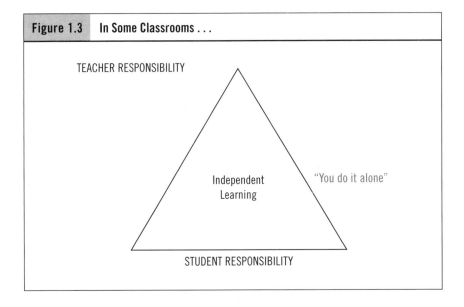

Figure 1.3   In Some Classrooms . . .

The structure of these classes is depressingly uniform. Students complete the prepared study packet of photocopied worksheets, or they read the assigned pages and then answer the questions at the back of the textbook—and they follow this pattern over and over again, day after day. There really isn't much teaching going on in these classrooms; it's mostly assigning or *causing* work. Frankly, we'd be embarrassed to cash our pay-checks if we "taught" like this.

There are days at school when students do need to spend significant amounts of time working independently—completing projects, writing essays, and the like. However, this should not be happening every day, and on the days it does happen, students need to be reminded of the purpose of the lesson, experience a brief episode of expert thinking, and interact with their peers.

Even in classrooms that most people would consider "good" or "good enough," the gradual release of responsibility instructional framework is seldom fully operationalized. As noted, the most frequent omission is the collaborative learning phase, leading to the instructional approach represented in Figure 1.4.

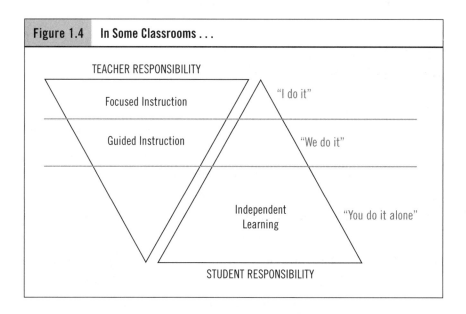

Figure 1.4   In Some Classrooms . . .

TEACHER RESPONSIBILITY

Focused Instruction

"I do it"

Guided Instruction

"We do it"

Independent Learning

"You do it alone"

STUDENT RESPONSIBILITY

In these classrooms, the teacher provides modeling and then meets with small groups of students. But students don't have the opportunity to collaborate, as they are all required to complete independent tasks while waiting their turn to meet with the teacher. For example, the teacher might model comprehension strategies useful in understanding scientific texts (*I do it*) and then meet with two or three small groups of students to guide their understanding (*We do it together*). As this is going on, the rest of the students are more likely to be assigned independent reading from a textbook (*You do it*) than they are to work in collaborative learning groups (*You do it together*).

We believe that all four phases of the gradual release of responsibility framework—focused instruction, guided instruction, collaborative learning, and independent learning—are necessary if we want students to learn deeply, think critically and creatively, and be able to mobilize learning strategies. But we didn't always understand this. Our teaching histories are replete with all of the ineffective models of instruction that we've just described.

When the Importance of Gradual Release Became Real for Us

The gradual release of responsibility instructional framework has been around for decades, and we have long used it with both the education students in our preservice classes and our public school students. But we can remember very specifically when we fully grasped its importance. The two of us were in Las Vegas at a conference. We were staying at the Venetian Hotel, a very nice place to stay. Doug had a cell phone on his hip, the old kind of cell phone that did one thing only—it made phone calls.

While we were walking through the lobby, Doug's phone rang. As he tried to answer it, it fell from his hip into the Venetian's lagoon, and down the drain it went. Given that Doug couldn't imagine a weekend without a cell phone (even one that couldn't do anything fancy), we took a taxi to the local Sprint store. Doug's plan was to exercise his insurance policy and get a free replacement phone.

The salesperson at the Sprint store saw the situation differently. Wanting to make a new sale, he directed Doug away from the "old school" phones and toward the new, high-tech models. "You need a phone that is more intuitive," he told Doug. "One that has e-mail, an address book, a calendar program, and that can search the Web." Doug assured him that no, he did not need any of these things. The sales guy—we'll call him Steve—was very persistent and noted that the newer phones also sent text messages. Doug had never sent a text message in his life, nor had the need ever arisen. But Steve was skilled. He said, "You know, the young people all send text messages. It's the new way of communicating." Doug wants to be a young person, so out came his credit card. Within minutes, he was the proud owner of a Treo 650. As Doug watched, Steve the salesperson demonstrated the phone's various fancy features. Doug felt pretty proud of his high-tech purchase.

About an hour later, back at the hotel, the new phone rang. There it sat, buzzing away, but Doug didn't know how to answer it. It didn't flip open like his old phone had, and there wasn't any obvious button labeled "Answer." Frustrated, we both got back in the taxi and returned to the Sprint store.

Of course, Doug couldn't bear to tell Steve the sales guy (who seemed to be about 12 years old) that he didn't know how to work the phone. He just held it up and said, "I think it's broken." Steve immediately took it out of Doug's hand and started working the phone.

Doug was suddenly struck by a wave of guilt. Turning to Nancy, he said, "How many times have I modeled comprehension for my students only to take back the task when they had difficulty?" What Steve the sales guy did, and what Doug recognized as something he was prone to doing himself, is a violation of the gradual release of responsibility instructional framework. When learners experience difficulty and confusion, they need guided instruction, not more modeling. Frustrated learners already know that their teachers can complete the tasks; they've seen their teachers do so several times over. What a frustrated learner needs is direction and practice, with scaffolding in place to ensure success.

Back at the store, Doug turned to Steve and said, "I really don't need another model. I need some guided instruction. Can I hold the phone while you talk me through the operation?" Steve was a little puzzled, but he obliged. He guided, prompted, questioned, and cued Doug on how to use the phone. (Nancy got so caught up in the experience that she decided, on the spot, to buy a new Treo 650 as well.)

Of course the combination of focused instruction and one guided instructional event did not ensure that either of us could use our new technology independently. What we needed now was the opportunity to practice without the teacher (in this case, Steve) providing cues. As Doug said to Nancy, "I'm too embarrassed to ask him how to do it again. We'll have to figure it out." Well, figure it out we did, slowly and over time. That night at dinner at the Capitol Grill, we sat across the table from one another sending text messages. We collaborated, problem solving as we went.

Over several weeks, with much practice and peer support, we both incorporated this new technology into our lives. And the process helped us grasp, definitively, that everything we know how to do well, we learned through this process of modeling, guided practice, collaborative learning, and independent application. The gradual release of responsibility instructional framework became real to us then, and we've both used and advocated for it ever since.

Conclusion

Structured teaching requires that teachers know their students and content well, that they regularly assess students' understanding of the content, and that they purposefully plan interrelated lessons that transfer responsibility from the teacher to the student. The theory that guides this type of teaching, the gradual release of responsibility, can also be conceptualized as shown in Figure 1.5, which highlights the framework's recursive structure

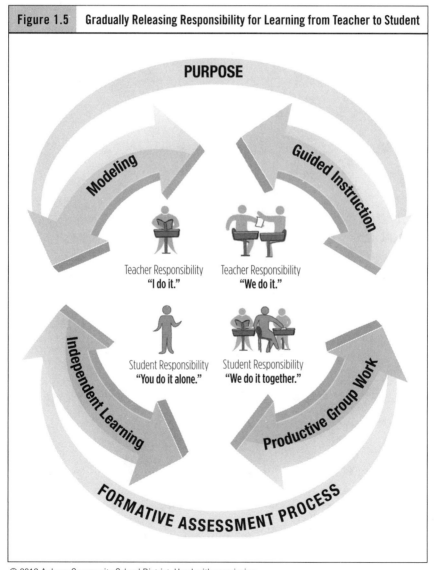

Figure 1.5 **Gradually Releasing Responsibility for Learning from Teacher to Student**

PURPOSE

Modeling

Guided Instruction

Teacher Responsibility
"I do it."

Teacher Responsibility
"We do it."

Student Responsibility
"You do it alone."

Student Responsibility
"We do it together."

Independent Learning

Productive Group Work

FORMATIVE ASSESSMENT PROCESS

and the ways in which teachers might vary its four instructional phases to optimize learning.

In the remainder of this book, we examine each aspect of this instructional framework and note the variations that teachers can use to meet students' needs.

Focused Instruction:
Purpose, Modeling,
Think-Alouds, and Noticing

Imagine learning to drive a car without ever having seen a car in motion. The sensory input alone would be enough to overwhelm the student driver, and the chaos of unfamiliar buttons, sounds, and movement would quickly lead to failure. The driving instructor would be equally dismayed. How can one teach a complex skill like driving if the learner has no concept of its purpose and how it should look?

In too many classrooms this is exactly what occurs. Students are told a lot of facts, and then they are expected to apply these facts flawlessly. Those who regularly fail at this application risk having their character, work habits, or intelligence called into question. Teachers need to acknowledge that what we teach is complex for the learner even if it is comparatively easier for us. Furthermore, teachers need to recognize that a learner who understands the purpose of a new skill and gets an opportunity to see it executed by an expert is going to grasp the details more thoroughly.

Focused instruction is not the time when a teacher simply *tells* students things—in fact, there's no time in teaching when "just telling" is enough. The key to quality teaching is *explaining*. Students need an explanation of their teachers' cognitive processes and metacognitive thinking. Learning theorists variously call this *direct explanation* or *cognitive strategies instruction*. However it is labeled, the intended goal is for the learner to encounter both the content and "the collection of mental tactics employed by an individual in a particular learning situation to facilitate acquisition of knowledge or skill" (Derry & Murphy, 1986, p. 2). As we discussed in Chapter 1, people don't really learn from being told. Learners need scaffolds and supports to process information, a fact that has implications for every classroom.

As teachers, we should continually ask ourselves if we are *explaining* or *simply telling*. This question has profound implications, especially for lectures in middle and high school. A good lecture lets the learners in on the teacher's thinking and does not simply regurgitate information that they could have read. What students do not need is an "information dump" from teacher to student. A good lecture also models critical thinking, as the "teacher questions her own assumptions, acknowledges ethical dilemmas hidden in her position, refers to inconvenient theories, facts, and philosophies that she has deliberately overlooked, and demonstrates an openness to alternative viewpoints" (Brookfield, 1995, p. 19). Finally, the worthwhile lecture, while brief in nature, conveys new terms and concepts and draws connections between ideas.

There is wide agreement that the Common Core State Standards for Mathematics and for English Language Arts and Literacy in History/Social Studies, Science, and Technical Subjects (NGA/CCSSO, 2010a, 2010b) call for higher learning expectations. Many educators are concerned about their ability to get students to the levels expected. After all, some teachers feel they are having a hard time getting students to achieve the *current* standards. But the shift from state standards to the Common Core is more than just an embrace of rigor; it's a move from teaching facts to teaching thinking. Teachers today are defining themselves less as dispensers of knowledge and more as facilitators of critical thinking, reasoning, and argumentation. We know that if we want our students to engage in critical thinking, we must be critical thinkers ourselves.

The purpose of this chapter is to examine the instructional moves that focus a student on the content, strategies, or skills being taught. These instructional moves—*establishing purpose, modeling or demonstrating,* and *thinking aloud*—are vital in preparing students for learning. Although we will discuss them as separate concepts in order to examine each in more detail, in practice, focused instruction combines several of these elements at any given moment. A fourth instructional move during focused instruction occurs in the mind of the teacher: *noticing.* This is the practice of expert teachers who watch carefully for student learning as the cognitive responsibility begins to shift from teacher to learner. Noticing is analogous to what a coach does as she scrutinizes an athlete's attempt at a new technique. The coach isn't just standing idly by; she is watching carefully. She will use what she notices to decide what next step will best develop the athlete's skills. Noticing is the linchpin between focused and guided instruction.

As we discussed in Chapter 1, the amount of responsibility the teacher and student bear varies during each of these instructional moves. This division of responsibility, though, should not be misinterpreted as a specific way of allotting or organizing time within a lesson. Focused instruction involves establishing purpose, modeling or demonstrating, thinking aloud, and noticing. Although this segment is often brief in nature, it is powerful—the time when the teacher uses the students' attention to introduce the concept, skill, or strategy they are to learn and executes key instructional moves designed to make what is being taught transparent to the learner. This notion of transparency is critical in the focused instruction phase. In order for students to acquire new knowledge, they need to understand the purpose and the learning target. They need to witness a more knowledgeable other (typically, the teacher) utilize the strategy being demonstrated, and they need to be invited into the mind of that more knowledgeable other. Teachers issue this invitation by sharing their thinking—clarifying for students not only the task process overall but also how to tackle the decisions necessary to the successful completion of the task. Finally, students need a knowledgeable teacher who will closely observe their early attempts and continue to coach and scaffold.

The Folly of Skipping the Focused Instruction Phase

Because this phase is relatively short, it can be tempting to hurry through it, dispensing some facts and doling out some directions. As one teacher asked, "Do we always need to give students a reason for everything? Shouldn't they just have to read because we told them to?" Although the "just because" reason can be enough if the desired outcome is compliance, the goal of school should always be learning. Telling students *what* they will be doing but not *why* and *how* and *when* and *when not* presumes a tremendous amount of motivation and skill. Some students may learn well enough without *whys, hows, whens,* and *when nots,* but many more will not.

One element of focused instruction is establishing the purpose, ensuring that students are informed about what they are learning *today* and how they will be applying this knowledge *today.* Establishing a purpose is different from sharing an agenda (which can also be done), as an agenda typically focuses on the order of the tasks students will be completing—the *what*s alone. Conveying the purpose of the lesson alerts students to expectations as it primes them for the content. There is a deep well of research backing up the fact that when the learning target is clear, the learner is more likely to successfully achieve it (see Hattie, 2009; Wiliam, 2007).

The second dimension to establishing purpose, one that is often overlooked, has to do with motivation. The fact is that few things are as motivating as success. No one likes to be confronted by failure over and over. (It's why Nancy gave up on learning how to ski.) But when we succeed in something, we are more likely to continue to engage in it for the good feelings that success gives us. It's not mastery that is motivating so much as visible progress toward a goal. Establishing a clear learning target and making sure students know what is expected of them and how it will be achieved builds incremental success and motivates students to continue their pursuit.

Another reason it's risky to skip the focused instruction phase is because doing so presumes students have a handle on the internal decision making that occurs in the mind of an expert as he or she processes information. In our experience, this isn't the case at all; if anything, students tend to believe, incorrectly, that an expert's thinking is always assured, linear, and unswerving. When they gaze on their algebra teacher as he completes a quadratic equation, they can't see that, inside his head, he is rapidly entertaining and discarding possible ways to factor, isolate the coefficients, and such. All they see is the teacher flawlessly executing yet another difficult problem. "How can I possibly do this?" they wonder, and for too many, the answer is either "I can't" (because they don't get it and figure they must be stupid) or "I won't" (because they don't get it, and algebra is stupid, and why should they bother?). Student motivation goes down, and often students' heads go down too, to rest on their open math books. (Maybe osmosis will work?) The thinking aloud that accompanies focused instruction's modeling, demonstrating, and direct explanations allows students to witness the "decision-making tree" experts create and follow as they engage with complex ideas and processes.

Key Features of Focused Instruction

We have talked a little already about the four features of focused instruction: establishing purpose, modeling, think-alouds, and noticing. Now it's time to look at each in more detail and consider how to put these instructional moves in play.

Establishing Purpose

The first key feature of focused instruction is establishing a purpose for the learning. As we've discussed, establishing purpose—*setting objectives* (Dean, Hubbell, Pitler, & Stone, 2012)—is an instructional routine that matters. In the absence of explicit attention to the lesson's purpose, students will not see the connection between the activities they are completing (e.g., the tasks listed on the agenda) and the reasons why they are learning it (i.e., how, when, and where to apply it [Dean et al., 2012]). Similarly, Hill and Flynn (2006) suggest that establishing purpose is especially critical to the success of English language learners. When students are just learning the language their teacher is speaking, they don't always know what to pay attention to in class or what really matters.

Unfortunately, in many districts, the good idea of establishing purpose has been misapplied and reduced to the requirement that teachers post the standards associated with the lesson on the wall. Simply posting standards, be they Common Core or any other, will not make the purpose clear to students. Standards as written are simply too broad and, if posted day after day without comment, might as well be wallpaper. Students need to be involved in the process of establishing purpose, they need to talk about the purpose, and they need to understand the goals of the instruction. Students need a clear explanation of the lesson's purpose and a clear explanation of the activities that are linked to that purpose.

As we noted in Chapter 1, teachers can establish purpose in three domains: content, language, and social. The example in Chapter 1 was from a mathematics classroom. Consider the following example from a science classroom. The 4th grade teacher established purpose right after her students had responded to a writing prompt posted as their bellwork. The prompt read, "When a little kid asks me about a food chain, I will explain it like this. . . ." Then the teacher said,

> As you know or could predict from our writing prompt, we're still studying the food chain. Today, we're going to look at the primary source of matter and energy in the food chain—plants. We need to learn more about plants as a source of matter and energy so that we can understand the food chain better. In doing so, I want to be sure that we're paying attention to our key terms: *producers* and *consumers* such as *herbivores, carnivores, omnivores,* and *decomposers.* I also want to make sure that we remember to write in complete sentences, not fragments. And finally, our social goal for the week is to actively listen while others are speaking. To accomplish these things, I'll be reading and talking about plants with you and then you'll be reading, talking, and writing about them as well. Some of you will be on computers doing Internet research; others will be reading more about decomposers such as fungi, insects, and microorganisms that recycle matter from dead plants and animals; and still others will be watching a short film about this topic.

Notice where establishing purpose occurred in the lesson: after students had engaged in some independent learning. Keep in mind that the instructional moves we make in a gradual release of responsibility instructional framework are not strictly linear. An established purpose also makes checking for understanding clear, as both the students and the teacher know what will be accepted as evidence of learning with that lesson. It also serves as a means for reminding students what the learning targets are as they transition to another phase of the lesson, so that they don't lose the reason for learning because now they're attending to the activity directions. Finally, a return to the established purpose serves as a strong method for closing the lesson.

Modeling and Demonstrating

The second key feature of focused instruction is modeling or demonstrating. We think of *modeling* as an instructional move used when the lesson addresses using a cognitive process, such as reading, writing, mathematics, and such. *Demonstrating* is what a teacher does when focusing on physical tasks, such as the proper stance for swinging a baseball bat or the procedure for turning on a Bunsen burner.

Think of the times you have viewed an online video demonstration of a complicated process you were interested in learning. Whether it was a video on how to make a soufflé or the basic casts in fly-fishing, it was most likely accompanied by the narration of an expert who explained what he or she was doing. The combination of verbal and visual elements reinforces the important aspects of the task. The features of modeling and demonstrating are similar. Here they are, accompanied by an example of how a language arts teacher might model the process of sentence-combining:

1. *Name the strategy, skill, or task.* ("Today I am going to show you how to combine sentences to make more interesting and complex statements.")

2. *State the purpose of the strategy, skill, or task.* ("It's important for a writer to be able to construct sentences that aren't repetitive or choppy. Sentence-combining is one way to make sure your sentences read more smoothly.")

3. *Explain when the strategy or skill is used.* ("After I have written a passage, I reread it to see if I have choppy sentences or if I am repeating information unnecessarily. When I notice that's occurred, I look for ways to combine sentences.")

4. *Use analogies to link prior knowledge to new learning.* ("I like to think of this as making sure I make a straight path for my readers to follow. When I eliminate choppy or redundant sentences, it's like making a straight path of ideas for them to follow.")

5. *Demonstrate how the skill, strategy, or task is completed.* ("I'm going to show you three short, choppy sentences. I'll look first for information I can cross out because it is repetitive. Then I'm going to combine those three sentences into one longer and more interesting sentence.")

6. *Alert learners about errors to avoid.* ("I have to be careful not to cut out so much information that I lose the meaning. I also need to watch out for sentences that become too long. A reader can lose the meaning of a sentence that's too long.")

7. *Assess the use of the skill.* ("Now I'm going to reread my new sentence to see if it makes sense.")

Modeling or demonstrating is not simply showing; it is accompanied by spoken language designed to provide a narrative for the learner to follow. When learners have a skill or strategy modeled for them rather than told to them, they gain a deeper understanding for when to apply it, what to watch out for, and how to analyze their success. This is consistent with four dimensions of learning: declarative (*What is it?*), procedural (*How do I use it?*), conditional (*When and where do I use it?*), and reflective (*How do I know I used it correctly?*) (Angelo, 1991). You can also see elements of metacognition emerging in the modeling example. Students are not just being taught how to do something; they are being primed to analyze the success of their use of what they are learning.

Demonstrations are similarly appropriate for tasks that involve movement, coordination, or any complex physical component. As an example, consider Brenda Lattner, who has begun a watercolor painting unit with her middle school art class. She knows her students need to learn how to stretch their watercolor paper correctly in order to have a satisfactory result with their final product. She begins by naming all the materials she will need for the task, including the paper, art tape, clean water and two sponges, and a board for mounting the paper. Next, she talks through the process:

> The first thing I need to do is check to make sure I have the side of the paper I want to use facing up. I can paint on either side, but I like to use the rougher side of the paper because it seems to hold my paint better. I can run my hand over both sides of the paper to figure out which side is rougher. The paper needs to soak in the water for a few minutes, so I am going to place it in the pan and set the timer for three minutes. That way I won't forget. In the pan, I put *tepid* water, which means water that is around room temperature. Hot water can ruin the paper. While it is soaking, I'll cut the strips of tape I'll need to mount the paper on the board. I have to make sure that the tape isn't shorter than the length of each side. If it is, the paper will dry funny, and I'll have a big bubble in it.

After the timer rings, Ms. Lattner continues:

> I'm going to be careful as I lift the paper, because I want as much water as possible to drain off of it. I can't put a sopping wet paper on the board because it will take forever to dry.

She holds the paper above the pan to allow the excess water to drain, explaining what she is thinking and doing:

OK, I think that's as much water as I'm going to get off of the paper this way. I've been watching the amount of water dripping in the pan, and it has slowed down to almost nothing. I know I can get water off another way: I'm going to lay the paper down on the board and use this sponge to smooth it. I've checked the sponge to make sure it's clean, and now I'm going to run it across the paper, using long strokes. The sponge absorbs water as it smooths the paper. Now that the paper is smooth, I need to tape it down. This tape gets sticky on one side, but you need water to make it sticky. I use a brown sponge for wetting the tape, so that I never mix up my smoothing sponges with my taping ones. You know why? Because that sticky stuff from the tape gets on the sponge. If I accidentally use that sponge later for smoothing, I'll get it all over the paper, and the paper will be ruined.

Ms. Lattner places the tape on all four edges of the paper, affixes it to the wooden board, and continues:

Now it's done! It needs to dry overnight, and when I check it tomorrow, it will be very tight and smooth. As the paper dries, it contracts, which means it gets a bit smaller. The tape holds it in place, so the contraction of the paper stretches it tight. When I paint on it, the surface will be smooth, and it won't crinkle up as I apply the watercolors to it.

This demonstration includes not only the sequence of steps but also insights into how to decide when it's time to go on to the next step. You may have noticed Ms. Lattner carefully noting the errors to avoid when completing this task. These verbal protocols, more commonly called think-alouds, are the third key feature of focused instruction.

Think-Alouds

The key to an effective think-aloud is to use the first person to describe how to make decisions, implement skills, activate problem-solving approaches, and evaluate whether success has been achieved. Duffy (2009) refers to think-alouds as "letting [students] in on the secret" to successfully completing a task (p. 50). They give students the opportunity to witness how an expert merges declarative, procedural, conditional, and reflective knowledge in a fluent fashion.

In a previous book of ours (Fisher & Frey, 2012c), we describe five key considerations in crafting an effective think-aloud:

• *Keep the focus of the think-aloud brief.* It is easy to get carried away with a think-aloud and turn it into a rambling monologue of every thought that wanders through your head. Choose a short piece of written text, a single math word problem, or one example of a procedure. It is better to deliver a short but effective think-aloud than one that serves only to confuse the learner with too many details.

• *Pay attention to your own thinking processes as you design your think-aloud.* This is really very difficult when you are an expert at something. Nathan and Petrosino (2003) state that "well-developed subject matter knowledge can lead people to assume that learning should follow the structure of the subject-matter domain rather than the learning needs and developmental profiles of novices"—a phenomenon they call the "expert blind spot" (p. 909). In other words, when you've been very adept at something for a long time, it can be difficult to retrace your own learning footsteps to recall a time when this information was new to you. A successful think-aloud requires you to unpack your own thinking processes to understand how you arrive at understanding.

• *Find your authentic voice when you think aloud.* This approach requires lots of "I" statements, which can feel contrived when you first begin. As teachers, it seems more comfortable to tell students information, using lots of "you" statements. The problem with "you" statements is that our instruction reverts to direct explanation, rather than making expert thinking transparent. Resist adopting an overly academic voice. Your students will find it more helpful to hear you say, "Wow—when I first looked at this diagram of the solar system, I thought right away about what it didn't have in the illustration, like the asteroid belt and the dwarf planets," rather than "I analyzed the diagram for the visual information it contained and immediately noted the small solar system bodies it did not contain."

• *Think like the expert you are.* Keeping a think-aloud authentic doesn't mean you have to check your expertise at the door. As a content area expert, you have the ability to share unique insights with your students. Effective think-alouds give you the opportunity to think like the mathematician, scientist, artist, historian, athlete, or literary critic you are, in front of your students.

• *Name your cognitive and metacognitive processes.* Labeling is essential if students are to build their own metacognitive awareness. Tell students when you are using the associative property of multiplication or sourcing a primary source document in a history class; these are cognitive approaches you are teaching them to use. In addition, signal your own metacognition as you problem-solve ("OK, that didn't work, so I have to try a different formula"), acquire new knowledge ("Wow, that's something I didn't know until just now, reading this article"), and regulate your learning ("I know that I usually understand an editorial better when I know who's written it, so I always look at the writer's affiliation first").

Think-alouds have become a staple of secondary school classrooms, as teachers use the dense informational readings of the course as an opportunity to show students how to understand the content. Given the increased expectations of the Common Core State Standards, especially those related to argumentation and mathematical practices, it is more important than ever for teachers to think aloud on a regular basis.

An essential consideration with this approach is the students' access to the text. Many teachers project the reading so that students can follow along as the text is read, or they provide students with their own paper copy of the reading. However, in both of these situations, notice who is bearing the cognitive load: it is the teacher who is doing the reading, while students follow along silently. The teacher pauses throughout the reading to think aloud about the information, and to explain his or her own mental processes in understanding the text.

Now, an example. Craig Brownlee, a 10th grade biology teacher, has been teaching a unit about human immune response, and his students have been struggling with understanding the role of phagocytes in fighting disease. He reads aloud a passage: "Phagocytes destroy any foreign body, including the debris and dead cells produced by injury. They overwhelm the injured areas and engulf the foreign bodies through a process called phagocytosis." Mr. Brownlee knows this statement contains a number of concepts that are easily misunderstood, so he pauses to think aloud:

> When I first learned about phagocytes, I couldn't really get my head around what they did. Then my biology professor told me that *phagocyte* means "a cell that eats." That helped me understand a bit more. A phagocyte doesn't eat like we do, but it swallows up the garbage that shouldn't be there. There's a word in that sentence that confirms my recollection of that idea. The word *engulf* means "to swallow something up," "to surround it." Now I can connect that to one more idea in that sentence—phagocytosis. Anytime I see a word that ends in *-osis,* it's a signal to me that it is a process. So phagocytosis is the process used by a phagocyte, a cell that eats, to swallow up anything it thinks shouldn't belong there. I had to take that sentence apart to understand it, and I did it by analyzing the derivations of a science term, then confirming my understanding using other terms in the sentence.

Here, Mr. Brownlee is modeling how he understands this informational text as a biologist. He also is explicit in naming the strategies he activated, so as not to leave it to chance whether his students would notice (or not). Keep in mind a goal of the think-aloud is to let novices in on how an expert synthesizes skills and habits of mind. Another is to prime students to become more aware of their own thinking processes. This metacognitive awareness is essential in order for students to gain insight into their own learning, and it is invaluable during guided instruction and collaborative learning, when students are required to express their thinking in words.

Noticing

Noticing, the fourth key feature of focused instruction, is fundamental to teaching, so much so that the relative ability of a teacher to engage in this practice is an important determinant in identifying novice and expert teachers (Donovan & Bransford, 2005). In fact, we would argue that noticing is a definitive behavior in teaching. After all, any number of curriculum materials, such as the textbook or a video, can present information. They can easily be structured to include a clear purpose, excellent modeling, and effective think-alouds. But no curricula can notice what students do with the new learning and make rapid decisions about what should occur next; only an expert teacher can do that. Expert teachers recognize that noticing and interpreting their students' thinking reveals the relative effectiveness of prior instruction and informs their subsequent instructional decisions.

Noticing is not evaluating. Novice teachers tend to use a too simplistic measure: *Is the student right or wrong?* Evaluation, especially on these broad terms, is problematic because it can lead the teacher to reduce task complexity (so that it's not too hard to "get") rather than provide scaffolding to help students rise to the challenge. Choppin (2011) studied the practices of novice and expert middle and high school mathematics teachers to determine how their noticing practices affected subsequent teaching. In every case, the novice teachers reduced the complexity of the task by "narrowing the choices available for students and by minimizing opportunities for students to make connections by explaining their strategies and reflecting on other students' strategies" (p. 189). They justified their decisions by asserting that students just didn't get it. The expert teachers, on the other hand, "engaged students in mathematical communication, in terms of explaining their thinking and in terms of attending to other students' thinking" (p. 195). In one case, a teacher pressed for explanation and justification 18 times in a 30-minute period of whole-class instruction.

It is this teacher behavior that serves as the transition to guided instruction. You are observing, listening, and using your knowledge of the content, of novice learners, and of their likely misconceptions or partial understandings to help you formulate the questions, prompts, and cues you'll need to scaffold student learning when you transition into guided instruction.

Here's another example. In her geometry class, Tina Nguyen establishes the purpose of the lesson, which centers on measuring exterior angles of triangles. She also explains her language goal (to incorporate vocabulary into discussions and proofs) and social goal (to collaborate with peers in a group project). Before asking students to work in groups and solve problems and proofs, Ms. Nguyen models the process and accompanies it with her mathematical thinking. She reads the definition of the theorem: "The measure of an exterior angle of a triangle is equal to the sum of the measures of the two non-adjacent interior angles." She then explains her understanding of the theorem:

> I know that *sum* is "to add up." It's the answer when we add
> something up. I also know that *non-adjacent* means "not next
> to"; *non* means "not" and *adjacent* means "next to" or "near."

So, this theorem is saying to me that the measure of the exterior angle—this one [she points to an exterior angle]—is equal to the sum of the two that are not directly next to the exterior angle I'm trying to figure out. I also know that some people call the non-adjacent angles remote interior angles, but that doesn't really help me here.

Next, Ms. Nguyen looks at a problem: "In PQR, $m < Q = 45°$, and $m < R = 72°$. Find the measure of an exterior angle at P." Again, she shares her thinking through direct explanation:

OK, so I know that one angle is 45° and the other one is 72°. Wait, I don't have to do this in my head. It is always helpful to draw a diagram and label it with the given information. Let's see, I'll label the triangle with the degree angles, like this, and see if it helps. Yes, it does. Now I can see which are nonadjacent angles and which I need to solve. Easy! Now it's just a calculation problem. I'm ready for another.

Ms. Nguyen continues this way through two more examples and then invites students to try another problem using the small whiteboards on their desks. As they work, she watches for patterns to see where students are experiencing difficulty or success. She asks them to explain their solutions to a partner and listens to their discussions. In particular, Ms. Nguyen is listening for evidence that students are making connections to previously taught content. She is watching to see which students are using mathematical models to justify their answers. Most important, she is interpreting what she is seeing and hearing so she can decide whether to remain in the focused instruction phase or to move fully into guided instruction. She isn't evaluating or simply assembling a catalog of how many correct and incorrect solutions she sees. Rather, she is interpreting students' responses so that she will be able to further scaffold their understanding through appropriate questions, cues, and prompts (guided instruction).

As it happens, the students generate quite a few incorrect answers. A novice teacher might be tempted to scale back the complexity of the next problem, but Ms. Nguyen, an expert teacher, knows that student thinking is essential to learning complex material, and she knows that her role is to move them from informal to formal reasoning.

"We hung with this problem for at least 10 minutes," she noted afterward. "What's interesting is that over that period of time, I began to hear my own modeling and thinking aloud being enacted by them. Giving them that language, and that insight into how I think, really pays off when I see them beginning to apply similar rationales to explain their own thinking."

Formative Assessment During Focused Instruction

Every phase of instruction must be accompanied by a means of checking for understanding. In the focused instruction phase, this is often accomplished through oral and written summaries. With younger children, we usually have them "turn to a partner" to restate or summarize what they have just learned. We listen in on conversations and make notes of what we have overheard. Projecting these notes on a document camera, computer screen, or interactive whiteboard enables us to discuss the accuracy and completeness of the conversations ("Anthony and Tre said our classroom is a direct democracy because everyone has a vote, but our student council is a representative democracy because we elect leaders to vote for us"). This kind of group reflection on earlier partner talk is an excellent way to uncover what students understood (and misunderstood), which can provide direction for the next phase of instruction.

In addition to its value in formative assessment, partner talk allows us to promote social relationships among students, and it is particularly useful for English language learners who may be reluctant to participate in whole-class discussions. At the same time, it provides novices with an opportunity to use the academic language of the content in their retelling. For example, when Ms. Nguyen checked for understanding, she told students the terminology they needed to use in their explanation.

Finally, this procedure, reflecting on the group discussions, gives teachers a chance to build community in the classroom. We will often share the thinking of some of the quieter members of the class to build their social capital. Older students don't always appreciate the attention, so we usually place their comments anonymously. This lets them enjoy the recognition privately, while we still get to put good ideas out there in the class for everyone to consider.

A "ticket out the door" (Fisher & Frey, 2012c), written during the last few minutes of the class period and handed to the teacher on the way out of the classroom, is another means of checking student understanding during focused instruction. The teacher can quickly skim through the student-generated summaries to determine what, if anything, needs to be retaught the following day. The same strategy can be used with nonlinguistic representations of understanding, including drawings and diagrams. For example, Ms. Lattner, the art teacher, asked her students to illustrate the steps of stretching watercolor paper. After reviewing these illustrations to check for understanding, she returned them the following day so the students could use them as a reference when performing the task.

Conclusion

There are many ways to establish purpose, model thinking, demonstrate skills, and notice student thinking; we have listed only a few. During the focused instructional phase of the gradual release of responsibility model, concepts and skills are introduced to students through a series of instructional moves that begins with establishing the purpose. The teacher models or demonstrates the content, strategy, or skill. To promote metacognition, the teacher thinks aloud so that students can witness the thinking processes used to understand the concept or master the skill. Most important, the teacher engages in noticing in order to interpret student reasoning. The formative assessment conducted through this noticing is the transition to guided instruction. Collectively, these instructional moves define the learning target for the student and increase the likelihood of success.

Guided Instruction:
Questions, Prompts, and Cues

The guided instruction phase of the gradual release of responsibility instructional framework is the point where the cognitive load begins to shift from teacher to student. In guided instruction, the teacher begins to follow the lead of the learner, who is challenged to apply the skill or strategy presented in a new situation. It's not unlike teaching a child to ride a bicycle—specifically the stage when you are running alongside the novice rider, reaching out to steady her when she begins to wobble, and then letting go again after she has regained control. Knowing when to offer a steadying hand and when to withdraw it is truly the art and science of teaching.

During the guided instruction phase, the teacher focuses on scaffolding students' developing skill or knowledge through questioning, prompting, and cuing. Meanwhile, the other students in the class engage in collaborative learning (more on that in Chapter 4) or independent learning (the focus of Chapter 5). It's important to stress, however, that guided instruction is not the same thing as ability grouping. *Ability grouping,* a permanent structure in which specific students are grouped with peers based on perceived ability, is an ineffective approach to increasing student performance and can be damaging to students' self-esteem. Guided instruction is temporary, flexible, and responsive. There isn't a standard script to follow for a guided instruction lesson, because the teacher's actions are predicated on what the students say and do, and what that might reveal about the students' needs. For the teacher, this means maintaining a heightened sense of awareness and keeping up a stream of internal questions: *Does this student need a bit of reteaching before he is able to explain the differences between meiosis and mitosis? Is this group now ready to analyze a political cartoon critical of FDR's first 100 days in office because they understand the controversies of the time regarding government interference? Do I expect some students to have difficulty recognizing a scalene triangle when it is shown in a different orientation?*

In other words, guided instruction is not the same for every group, nor does it necessarily happen every day for every student. It's not likely that you will meet with every group on a daily basis, especially if you're teaching at the secondary level. Instead, you might meet with each group one to three times a week, depending on the length of the lessons. Some students need more guided instruction than others, so you will want to stack the deck a bit to meet with some groups more frequently. You also can alter the size of the groups, so that students who need more help are in groups with fewer members; this allows you more "face time" with them. Remember, though, that guided instruction should not be reserved for students who are struggling; those who perform at grade level but could be performing higher, as well as students who are advanced and need to be challenged, also deserve this type of targeted instruction and benefit from it.

Key Features of Guided Instruction

A hallmark of guided instruction is that the dialogue between teacher and learners is carefully crafted following the principles of *scaffolding*. This term was coined as a metaphor for describing the temporary supports, in the form of questions, prompts, and cues, a teacher offers learners as a bridge toward a skill or concept they cannot otherwise perform or grasp independently (Wood et al., 1976).

Try thinking of the guided instruction process in terms of a flowchart (see Figure 3.1). When one scaffold does not work, move on to the next. When the scaffold works, return to questioning to check for understanding or to probe deeper about students' knowledge.

Let's take a closer look now at the three major types of scaffolds.

Asking Questions

A basic assumption of guided instruction is that the students are responding in a perfectly logical manner given what they know and don't know at that particular moment. Therefore, the internal question a teacher should ask during this phase of instruction is this: *What does this child's answer tell me about what he knows and doesn't know?* Questions that check for understanding are very important during guided instruction, but questions that uncover errors and misconceptions are essential.

Asking students to elaborate or to clarify their answers allows you to determine how to respond and how best to scaffold understanding. For instance, if a student reads *horse* instead of *house,* this may be because

- The student may not be attending closely to the word;
- The student may not yet be attending to the medial position in the word; or

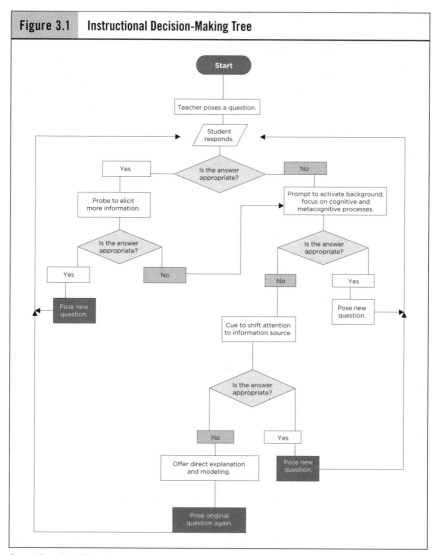

Figure 3.1   Instructional Decision-Making Tree

Source: Frey, N., & Fisher, D. (2010). Identifying Instructional Moves During Guided Learning. *The Reading Teacher,* 64(2). Copyright 2010 by the International Reading Association. Used with permission.

- The student may not be familiar with the vowel combination in the word.

That rapid hypothesis formulation must now be followed by a teacher response. For example:

- *If you think the student is not attending to print:* "Look again. Does that sound right?"
- *If you think the student is having difficulty with medial positions:* "You missed the middle sound. Look again at the middle letters, and try reading it again."
- *If you think the student is unfamiliar with the vowel combination:* "The letters *o* and *u* make the /*ow*/ sound. Try the word again using that sound."

The alternative to scaffolding, of course, is simple correction: "That word is *house*. Read it again, please." The problem with correction is that you don't get to test your hypothesis as to why the error was made. Scaffolding with prompts and cues gives you the chance to gain a better understanding of what the student knows and doesn't know so that you can take action to get learning back on track.

Prompts

There are a number of different things a teacher can say to engage learners in cognitive or metacognitive work. That's the key to a prompt: getting students to do some thinking. Figure 3.2 summarizes the different types of prompts.

Essentially, prompts are hints or reminders that encourage students to do the work when they have temporarily forgotten to use a known skill or strategy in an unfamiliar situation. Prompts can be phrased as statements or questions, but the teacher should not assume so much responsibility as to tell the student what information is missing. Instead, the prompt is designed to guide students' thinking. Over time, and with practice, students will begin to incorporate this type of thinking into their habits.

Here is a look at how prompting works. Ahmad Tarmizi is meeting with a group of students who generally perform at grade level but are not making much progress toward the mastery of Anchor

Figure 3.2	Prompt Types and Examples	
Type of Prompt	**Definition**	**Examples**
Background knowledge	Reference to content that the student already knows, has been taught, or has experienced but has temporarily forgotten or is not using correctly	• *When a student is trying to solve a right-triangle problem:* "I'm thinking about the total degrees inside a triangle." • *During a science unit about the water cycle:* "What do you remember about states of matter?"
Process or procedure	A reminder of established or generally agreed upon rules or guidelines that have been forgotten or are not being followed	• *When a student is pronouncing a word incorrectly:* "When two vowels go walking . . ." • *When a student gets the wrong answer from not following the order of operations:* "I'm thinking about a mnemonic that we use to remember the order for solving problems." • *When a student using a band saw accidentally breaks a board in two:* "Think about the role of the wood's grain. Remember the rule for that?"
Reflective	A reminder to students to be metacognitive and think about their thinking for the purpose of determining the next steps or the solution to a problem	• *When a student has just read something incorrectly:* "Does that make sense? Really think about it." • *When a student's writing does not include evidence, as the assignment required:* "What are we learning today? What was our purpose?"
Heuristic	Any informal problem-solving procedure suggested to help learners develop their own effective way to solve a problem	• *When a student does not get the correct answer to a math problem:* "Maybe drawing a visual representation would help you see the problem." • *When a student gets stuck and cannot think of what to write next:* "Writers have a lot of different ways for getting unstuck. Some just write whatever comes to mind, others create a visual, others talk it out with a reader, and others take a break and walk around for a few minutes. Will any of those help you?"

Standard 8 of the Common Core's English language arts (ELA) and literacy standards: "Gather relevant information from multiple print and digital sources, assess the credibility and accuracy of each source, and integrate the information while avoiding plagiarism" (NGA/CCSSO, 2010a, p. 41). As part of their conversation, Mr. Tarmizi uses prompts to guide his students' understanding:

Mr. Tarmizi: Which of these sources did your group rate as "credible and accurate"?

Dewa: All of them. They're all accurate. They all have statistics and information in them.

Ramzy: Yeah, they're credible, too.

Mr. Tarmizi: Why? I'm not saying that you're wrong; I just want to know how you reached that agreement. (questioning prompt)

Miguel: Well, because . . . I don't really know . . . they're all about the same topic.

Mr. Tarmizi: I'm thinking about the credibility tool we used a few weeks ago. There were items on that checklist. . . . (procedural prompt)

Dewa: Oh, yeah, look. They all have a copyright year!

Miguel: And there is a way to contact the author or publisher. So we could check that.

Mr. Tarmizi: Nice. Well done. Those are two important considerations. But also think about the author and what you know about the author. (background knowledge prompt)

Ramzy: We did that. We looked up the authors, and they have written other stuff about these topics. So I do think that they are credible. They seem like subject matter experts—Is that what it was called?

Cues

Sometimes prompts are not sufficient or there isn't a clear way to prompt the student. In these cases, a cue is called for. *Cues* shift the learner's attention. They are also more specific and direct than prompts, meaning the teacher bears more cognitive responsibility. We liken cueing to the sports commentator who uses instant replay and slow motion to get us to notice a particular technique: "Hey, look here! And look carefully." Figure 3.3 provides an overview of the different types of cues.

Figure 3.3	Cue Types and Examples	
Type of Cue	**Definition**	**Examples**
Visual	A range of graphic hints to guide students' thinking or understanding	• Highlighting areas within text where students have made errors • Creating a graphic organizer to arrange content visually • Asking students to take a second look at a graphic or visual from a textbook
Verbal	Variations in speech to draw attention to something specific or verbal "attention getters" that focus students' thinking	• "This is important . . ." • "This is the tricky part. Be careful and be sure to . . ." • Repeating a student's statement using a questioning intonation • Changing voice volume or speed for emphasis
Gestural	Body movements or motions to draw attention to something that has been missed	• Pointing to the word wall when a student is searching for the right word or the spelling of a word • Making a predetermined hand motion • Placing thumbs around a key idea in a text that the student is missing
Environmental	Use of the classroom surroundings or physical objects in the environment to influence students' understanding	• Keeping environmental print (the written text on classroom walls) current so that students can use it as a reference • Using algebra tiles or other manipulatives • Moving an object or person so that the orientation changes or the perspective is altered

Cues are a common feature of teaching, especially during whole-class instruction and the initial introduction of content. Within the gradual release of responsibility instructional framework, they play an essential role when students are struggling. Rather than simply tell students the answer or how to apply the learning, the teacher uses cues to make sure students are taking on responsibility and doing the work.

For example, when the students in Kelly McKee's class study World War I, she creates a number of language charts, a visual timeline, and a word wall so that students will have a number of cues readily available. As part of the lesson activities, students create graphic organizers of the content, including locations of the war, the people and countries involved, and the key terminology. When a group gets stuck with a review question, Ms. McKee can point them to the visual timeline, which helps them figure out their response. When another group has difficulty comparing the two world wars, she can direct them back to their graphic organizers and all the thinking about the content they have captured there.

Direct Explanations

Sometimes prompts and cues are not enough to resolve the errors and misconceptions that students have. When confusion lingers, the teacher needs to provide a direct explanation. As we noted in Chapter 2, this doesn't mean just correcting students and telling them the information that they missed. It's a matter of shifting guided instruction back into focused instruction. The teacher reestablishes the learning purpose, provides an explanation with modeling and think-alouds, and then asks questions or sets small challenges in order to monitor student understanding:

- "Can you now explain the idea to your partner?"
- "Can you tell me what I just said in your own words?"

- "I'm going to ask you the original question again, now that you know _____."
- "How about writing a short summary of this in your notebook so you'll remember?"

Of course, students may not fully grasp the content at this point and may need additional guided instruction to really master the information, but right now, with prompts and cues having failed to clear up student confusion, the teacher is working toward a more modest goal: allowing students to experience some success. Think of it this way: If you do not understand something, despite significant efforts on the part of another person, at some point you will begin to doubt *yourself,* not the person providing the instruction. You might even think of yourself as stupid, at least in this one particular area. Many of the students we meet who believe they are "not good" at math, reading, writing, and so on are victims of this kind of debilitating negative thinking. Just a little bit of the productive success they can achieve with appropriate scaffolding is often enough to reestablish a more positive learning outlook.

Guided Instruction in the Classroom

The major moves of guided instruction—questions, prompts, and cues—are useful in transferring responsibility to students while still providing appropriate scaffolds for learning. Now, we'll examine some of the different ways that teachers can integrate guided instruction into the classroom.

Guided Reading Instruction

While most of her kindergarten class works in collaborative groups or independently, teacher Darla Cotton calls five of her students to the reading table to read from the emerging-reader book *Dad* (Rigby, 2004). Each sentence begins "Dad is. . . ." Ms. Cotton has previously focused her instruction on left-to-right directionality, C-V-C words, and basic sight words. Now it's time for this group of students to apply these skills and strategies with unfamiliar text.

She directs individual children to begin "whisper reading," staggering start times so that they do not fall into a choral reading of the text. Ms. Cotton moves around the table, listening to each student read, pausing to ask questions or offer prompts when they encounter difficulty, and making anecdotal notes. She notices that the children have done well with moving across each page and have correctly used the pattern of the text.

After they finish, she asks them to retell what occurred in the story so that she can determine their comprehension. One student, David, stumbles in his retelling, so Ms. Cotton invites him to use the book to recall. She then asks about the last page—why was Dad sleeping? A minute or two of discussion among the children, with prompts from Ms. Cotton, and the group has arrived at a decision: Dad was sleeping because he was tired from doing so many activities all day. Satisfied that this group is progressing in using their emergent knowledge of phonics, sight words, concepts about print, and comprehension, she sends them back to their collaborative learning groups and reviews her notes about their progress. She will use what she has learned to develop the next lesson.

High school English teacher Matt Tangaroa has introduced the paradox as a literary device used by writers and storytellers throughout the world. He presented several statements for his focused instruction to model his thinking when encountering a statement that seems to contradict itself yet somehow reveals a deeper truth (such as "being cruel to be kind" or George Bernard Shaw's comment that "youth is wasted on the young"). He also demonstrated how he uses inferencing in order to unearth the unstated truth.

Now Mr. Tangaroa wants students to examine paradox in the context of poetry. He sits down with a group of six high school students and shows them a copy of a very short poem by John Donne (1572–1631):

> I am unable, yonder beggar cries,
> To stand, or move; if he say true, he lies.

Mr. Tangaroa formed this group of students based on assessment evidence showing they had difficulty making the kinds of inferences necessary to understand a paradox. To start, he asks them each to read the poem aloud and then has them discuss in pairs the poem's meaning and why the author would say that the beggar was a liar. Through prompts and cues, Mr. Tangaroa leads the six students to understand the unstated paradox. During their conversation, one of the students notes, "By speaking, the beggar was moving, and so he was lying."

Mr. Tangaroa later meets with another group of students—those his assessment data suggest are still confused by the concept of paradox and need additional instruction. This time, he decides to use the Robert Frost poem "Nothing Gold Can Stay." The first line's statement that "nature's first green is gold" is a more accessible paradox for students, as it does not use a Middle English style and refers to a more familiar phenomenon. Thanks to a clear learning target and formative assessment information, Mr. Tangaroa uses guided instruction to effectively teach the same reading skills to a range of learners.

Guided Writing Instruction

During guided instruction, students apply what they have learned from focused instruction and collaborative learning, with varying degrees of support from the teacher. Teachers often use sentence or paragraph frames to scaffold students' academic writing.

These frames, models, or templates help students internalize conventional structures (Fisher & Frey, 2007b).

Aida Allen uses paragraph frames to help her students internalize academic writing. As part of a unit of study on characters, Ms. Allen meets with a group of students who have been having difficulty with character summaries and analysis. She presents a paragraph frame (see Figure 3.4) to her students and asks them to read it aloud, adding information orally based on the different books they have been reading.

As she listens to her students, she stops individual students and provides additional cues and prompts. For example, as Arturo suggests details about a character named Marty from *Shiloh*

Figure 3.4   Character Analysis Paragraph Frame

_____ is one of the characters in the story. _____ is

_____ and lives _____ (With whom? Where?).

At the beginning of the story, _____ is _____, but _____

who _____. _____

faces a problem when _____

_____ .

_____

_____ .

_____ attempts to solve the problem by _____

_____

but _____ .

Finally, _____ is able to solve the problem by _____

_____ .

At the end of the story, _____ has learned that _____

if _____ , then _____

_____ .

(Naylor, 1991), Ms. Allen asks him to list words to describe Marty as he was at the beginning of the story. Arturo says that Marty was shy and that he played by himself all the time. In response to her question about what else he remembers about Marty, Arturo shrugs his shoulders. She prompts him by saying, "Well, Marty was always looking around for things. What does that tell us about his personality?" Arturo and Ms. Allen agree that Marty was curious. Ms. Allen then turns her attention to Isabel, who isn't sure what her character, Esperanza from *Esperanza Rising* (Ryan, 2000), had learned. After the group completes the task of reading the paragraph frame aloud and adding details from their books, Ms. Allen asks them to use the frame to construct a paragraph in their journals. Here's what Arturo writes:

> Marty is one of the characters in the story. He is 8 years old and lives with his family in a house in the country. At the beginning of the story, Marty is a curious but shy boy who likes to play by himself. Marty is faced with a problem when he finds a stray dog. He knows who the dog belongs to and does not want to return him. He attempts to solve the problem by lying to his family and friends, but then he is caught. Finally, he is able to solve the problem by working hard and treating the dog's owner with respect. At the end of the story, he has learned that if you are honest and treat others with respect, then people will respect you.

Guided writing and the use of frames, models, and templates are not limited to the elementary school classroom. College composition experts Gerald Graff and Cathy Birkenstein (2009) recommend the use of frames (they call them templates) as an effective way for developing students' academic writing skills:

> After all, even the most creative forms of expression depend on established patterns and structures. Most songwriters, for instance, rely on a time-honored verse-chorus-verse pattern,

and few people would call Shakespeare uncreative because he didn't invent the sonnet or dramatic forms that he used to such dazzling effect. . . . Ultimately, then, creativity and originality lie not in the avoidance of established forms, but in the imaginative use of them. (pp. 10–11)

Guided Instruction with Student Think-Alouds

Think-alouds are commonly thought of as a teacher-directed instructional practice, as we discussed in Chapter 2. Indeed, it is a powerful tool for making thinking transparent to a group of learners. However, the real goal of thinking aloud is to prepare students to surface their own thinking processes as they learn and understand a new concept.

Student think-alouds are conducted in much the same way as teacher think-alouds. As students read a piece of text or perform a task, they pause to explain their thinking, including decisions they are making about what to do next. Student think-alouds are ideally suited for guided instruction, as they provide an opportunity to listen to the thinking processes of your students as they engage in new learning.

Lauren McDonnell's 6th grade history students had been introduced to the Code of Hammurabi during her focused instruction. When Ms. McDonnell read their "ticket out the door" written summaries at the end of class, she noticed that several of her students had difficulty explaining the pros and cons of the laws of ancient Babylon. She decided to meet with this group to review excerpts from their textbook, asking them to think aloud as they read. She hoped that by doing this she would gain insight into their reasoning.

Ms. McDonnell begins by distributing the text and quickly reviews the significance of this earliest preserved record of law, asking the students to think aloud about their impressions of fairness as they read. At Ms. McDonnell's request, Alex reads the portion of the code containing the *lex talionis,* better known as "an eye for an eye, a tooth for a tooth":

> *Ms. McDonnell:* Stop there, Alex, and tell me how you understand that term.
>
> *Alex:* Well, I guess I've got this picture in my head of a judge taking someone's eyeball out because the other guy lost his. Pretty gross.

Ms. McDonnell encourages Alex to read on and continue thinking aloud. Alex reads that the law only applies to injuries suffered by a free man, not enslaved people or children:

> *Alex:* I'm thinking that that doesn't seem very fair, like some people don't count. Girls and stuff. Shouldn't there be an "eye for an eye" rule for everyone?
>
> *Ms. McDonnell:* What did you do there just now? When you were thinking aloud?
>
> *Alex:* I asked myself a question about being fair.
>
> *Ms. McDonnell:* Exactly! That's how you start to form opinions about pros and cons. Make a note about that on your T-chart. Ricardo, how about if you think aloud about the next section, about family laws?

The students continue in this fashion for the next 10 minutes, reading parts of the text and commenting aloud about their thought processes. At the end of the lesson, each student has some ideas noted for the pros and cons of the Code of Hammurabi, and they will be able to return to their collaborative learning groups to contribute to a project on the importance of these laws on civilization.

Guided Instruction Through Close Reading

Close reading is another form of guided instruction. It is often done with the whole class but also can be implemented with smaller groups of students. Close reading provides students an opportunity to try on some of the things that they have learned and practiced in other phases of the gradual release of responsibility instructional framework. The key features of close reading include

- Focus on a complex, worthy text;
- Repeated reading of the entire text and portions of the text;
- Annotation of the text while reading, including underlining key ideas, circling words or phrases that are confusing, writing questions in the margins, and summarizing and synthesizing information in the margins;
- Text-dependent questions that require students to produce evidence from the text as part of their responses; and
- Extensive discussions between students about the text under investigation (Fisher & Frey, 2012a).

During close readings of complex text, the teacher uses scaffolds but avoids front-loading or preteaching vocabulary. In other words, instead of relying on "front-end scaffolds," students use scaffolds distributed throughout the instruction in the form of questions, prompts, and cues. Some "back-end scaffolds" might also be provided for students who still need instruction following the close reading.

Let's look at an example. Ninth grade English teacher Dustin Bradshaw used "Death of a Pig," a short story by E. B. White (1948), to introduce his students to close reading. On their first reading of the text, which centered on the first five paragraphs, Mr. Bradshaw asked the students to focus on the following questions and to use their annotation skills as they read:

- What is this passage mainly about?
- How is the passage organized?
- What words or phrases stand out to me as I read?
- Have I used structural and contextual analysis to resolve unknown words and phrases?

After reading the excerpt, the students, in their table groups, briefly discussed what they found. Mr. Bradshaw listened in on his students' conversations and was pleased to note that they generally understood the text and its organization.

Over the next several days, he asked students to reread the text and discuss their thinking about various text-dependent questions with their peers. Mr. Bradshaw developed significantly more text-dependent questions than he actually used. As he noted, "I keep a lot of different questions in my back pocket for when their conversations falter. I really want them to talk about all of these things, but sometimes a just-right question is needed to restart their thinking and talking." See Figure 3.5 for a list of his questions.

At one point on the second day of the close reading, Mr. Bradshaw noted that students were not picking up on the author's use of personification. He reminded the class of this literary device, providing them with two examples, which he displayed on the document camera:

> "The house sighed with sadness." This communicates the idea that the house is gloomy looking, or not completely stable. And here's another: "As he devoured the carcass, the vulture laughed with delight." I'd say the image of the vulture is enriched with the idea that it laughs in a sinister way. Including that phrase makes the vulture seem more evil than it might otherwise.

Mr. Bradshaw then asked the students to reread the text, considering the author's use of personification. They quickly got to work in their groups to find examples of personification:

Figure 3.5	Sample Text-Dependent Questions for Close Reading

Text: E. B. White's "Death of a Pig"

General Understandings
- Who is the narrator? What is his job?
- What is the conflict presented in Section 1 of this essay?
- Who are the characters? Describe them.

Key Details
- Is the narrator sick?
- What is the end result of the "first degree"?
- What is the pig's reaction to the oil?
- What is the dog compared to in Section 2?
- What is the narrator's community like?
- In Section 2, how do we know the pig is sick?
- How is the pig buried? Why is this significant?

Structure
- What is the extended metaphor being set up? What is the purpose?
- Locate areas of personification. What is the effect?
- What is the time sequence of the essay?
- Locate areas where the tone of the essay shifts. What is the purpose for this shift?
- Locate areas of foreshadowing. What event is being hinted at?

Vocabulary
- How is the term *scheme* defined?
- What are the people on the farm referred to as? Why?
- How is the treatment of the pig defined?
- What is the pig referred to as?

Author's Purpose
- How does the narrator link his own experiences with that of the pig?
- Does the narrator care about his pig? For what reasons?
- In Section 3, what does the pig's death represent?
- How do the narrator's emotions change in Section 3?
- What makes the pig's burial more "decent" than a human one?

Inferences Across the Text
- How does the narrator's attitude toward the dog change throughout the text?
- What ties the pig and the narrator together?
- By the end of the text, how does the narrator feel about his original plan for the pig? Cite specific evidence to support your thinking.

Cindy: In "The Pig," Section 2, he says, "In the upset position the corners of his mouth had been turned down, giving him a frowning expression." See, that is making us think that the pig has human characteristics.

Roel: In the dog section it says, "Ours was a businesslike procession, with Fred, the dishonorable pallbearer, staggering along in the rear, his perverse bereavement showing in every seam in his face." I think that's what we're looking for, because really the dog could not be sad because of the pig dying.

Guided Instruction with Misconception Analysis

The National Research Council's meta-analysis of practices that make a difference in history, mathematics, and science instruction for secondary students yielded three main recommendations:

• Teachers must know and anticipate misconceptions students possess about the concepts being taught.
• Educators must teach for factual knowledge in a systematic way.
• Students must be taught to be metacognitively aware of their learning (Donovan & Bransford, 2005).

A rich research record supports the importance of anticipating misconceptions (e.g., Guzzetti, Snyder, Glass, & Gamas, 1993). For example, young children may believe that multiplication always yields a larger number and, thus, become confounded when faced with multiplying fractions. Science students may hold the misconception that the Earth is at the center of the universe, or they may confuse acceleration and speed. A teacher who has anticipated misconceptions can address them during focused instruction—by using math manipulatives to show what occurs with fractions, for example, or by demonstrating a series of experiments on a skateboard to highlight the difference between speed

and acceleration. Of course, not all misconceptions can be anticipated; they may only surface during guided instruction, when the
teacher has a chance to hear students' reasoning.

Consider this scenario: Robert Sanchez has been working
with his science class on the concept of volume and has asked
a small group of students to explain what occurs when he does
a series of demonstrations for them. He asks them to create a
definition of *volume,* and he records their explanation that volume is the amount of space something takes up. He then places
a heavy block into a pan of water filled to the top and asks the
six students to discuss why some water spilled over the edge.
Their discussion is on target, as all of them are able to describe
the displacement effect. He then asks how they would measure
the volume of the block, and Antonio immediately says, "You
have to multiply! It's length times width times height!" The others nod in agreement, and soon they have calculated the volume
of the block.

Next, Mr. Sanchez asks the group to predict what will occur
when he repeats the experiment with objects of varying size,
all irregularly shaped. Again, they are able to explain that each
object displaced a different amount because the amount of space
it took up varied. Then he asks them how to calculate the volume
of an object, and the group falls quiet.

> *Mr. Sanchez:* OK, let's think about it for a moment. What do
> you know so far?
>
> *Claudia:* That the water has to go somewhere, and it gets
> pushed out of the pan.
>
> *Maureen:* We know how to do the math. We multiply the width
> and the length and the height.
>
> *Antonio:* I think we need to measure the object, just like we
> did with the block.

Mr. Sanchez hadn't expected this; he had thought the students would surmise that measuring the amount of water displaced would give them the information they needed. But he allows them to wrestle with this problem for several minutes, knowing that they need to conclude on their own that their methodology is flawed. He asks them questions from time to time, scaffolding their understanding of the problem they created for themselves. Claudia is the first to arrive at the notion that they could use the water to determine the volume of an irregularly shaped object. Mr. Sanchez then resumes the lesson he had originally planned, coaching the group through the process of measuring the water. However, because this group had more difficulty than he had expected, he asks them to write a short explanation of why their first idea did not work rather than a description of the experiment, which was his original plan. He uses their writing to check for understanding and to plan for his next guided instruction group with these students.

Guided Instruction, Differentiated

As Tomlinson and Imbeau (2010) point out, a teacher can differentiate content, process, and product. The guided instruction phase of the gradual release of responsibility instructional framework allows for differentiation of all three components. Keep in mind when differentiating that it should be done in service of moving students upward on a staircase of complexity.

Content. During small-group guided instruction, teachers can change the texts students are reading. They can change the mathematics problems students are expected to complete. They can vary the rate of learning expected or extend the content for some students beyond what others are learning, allowing for an enriched curriculum for those who have already mastered grade-level or course expectations. It is not assumed that the same students will always participate in accelerated learning or will need the text difficulty reduced; these instructional decisions are predicated on formative assessment data. One way to ensure that the same students aren't grouped the same way for every unit is to include interest groups as part of guided instruction.

Process. Differentiating process during guided instruction means adjusting activities. For example, teachers can vary the types of prompts used, based on student needs or strengths. They can vary the kinds of questions they ask or the level of support they provide. They can increase or decrease the visual support that is provided or encourage peer "language brokers" to talk with one another in their home language. Some students may benefit from encountering content via audio books, and others, from having content introduced to them before it is introduced to the large group so that they will have prior knowledge to draw upon. We have personally had great success offering "previews of coming attractions" in the form of graphic organizers or other visual displays so that learners possess a general schema in advance of the unit.

Products. The products that students generate as part of guided instruction are the record of their developing skills and understanding and extremely valuable for formative assessment. Teachers differentiate products in order to provide students with the best vehicle for showing what they know and can do. For some students, a conversation with the teacher does the trick. Others need to read and write. For still others, a performance or project might be the best approach.

The key to differentiating products is to create a menu of options. Teachers can chose which product they believe will best allow students to demonstrate mastery, or they can allow students to make that choice for themselves, with consultation and encouragement to stretch beyond their comfort zone. In the latter arrangement, a teacher might categorize product options according to type and then require each student to complete at least one from each category over the course of the semester:

- Oral language (e.g., meet with the teacher, tutor a classmate);
- Written language (e.g., essay, write a lesson plan, create a poem);
- Performance (e.g., deliver a public speech, write and perform a skit); and
- Project (e.g., research a topic, create a visual representation or model).

When students chose the product they will generate during guided instruction, they are grouping themselves according to that category, an interest group of sorts. It's just one of many ways that integrating the components of differentiated instruction and guided instruction allows us to be more responsive to each student's needs, strengths, and interests.

Formative Assessment During Guided Instruction

As part of guided instruction, students are grouped and regrouped based on their performance, not on the teacher's perception of their ability. The most effective guided instruction is based on formative assessment that is directly linked with content standards. For example, if the class is studying literary devices, the formative assessment data gathered might include a student's ability to recognize these devices and to use these devices when writing. Assessment results could be used to form groups based on identified needs (for example, one group that needs further instruction in the difference between foreshadowing and flashback, and another group that needs additional instruction in using personification to humanize something not human).

As we have stated, it's critical to check for understanding and provide course correction (the steadying hand on the bicycle) as students begin to take on new concepts, skills, and strategies. Some of the ways teachers might gather formative assessment data were covered in the examples earlier in the chapter, but let's augment those techniques with a few more.

Reading instruction. In her guided instruction, kindergarten teacher Darla Cotton used anecdotal notes and observations as she listened to her students read. Another technique that's useful with emergent and early readers is the running record, a system for recording the reading behaviors used during an oral reading (see Clay, 2000). Analyzing this written record later helps highlight the systems a child is using well, partially, or not at all, especially as they relate to knowledge of letters and sounds, the syntactic structure of the language, and meaning cues.

For older readers, teachers can administer commercially prepared grade-level informal reading inventories several times per year. However, although this kind of periodic data can be useful, it does not provide the immediate feedback needed to check for understanding. Retellings are an excellent tool for measuring the extent to which a student has comprehended the reading. Retelling rubrics are included in many reading programs and are often a part of a district's bank of informal assessments.

Writing instruction. Guided instruction in writing yields a permanent product, which serves as a great information source on students' status. Again, holistic or trait-specific rubrics are useful for analyzing writing. Because it can be unwieldy to analyze every piece of writing, we teach our students at the beginning of the year how to use student-friendly rubrics to score their own writing. Student rubrics help to build a learner's understanding of the expectations and measures of success that need to be internalized. Student self-scoring also increases metacognition, as learners are able to witness their gains over time (Fisher & Frey, 2007b).

Think-alouds. Student think-alouds are a bit trickier to assess because the product—talking—is so transient. The best way to get a snapshot of student understanding from a think-aloud is to prepare a checklist (see Figure 3.6) covering what you are listening for (the purpose, such as reading comprehension strategies or critical-thinking skills). As students think aloud, you can note

Figure 3.6	Checklist for Assessing a Student Think-Aloud	
Student Name:		**Date:**
Comprehension	Did the student . . . ❑ Make connections to other texts? ❑ Visualize? ❑ Question the text? ❑ Make inferences beyond the text? ❑ Determine importance of information? ❑ Summarize?	Notes/examples:
Content knowledge	Did the student . . . ❑ Activate background knowledge? ❑ Use word derivations? ❑ Use context clues? ❑ Use resources? ❑ Apply new knowledge?	Notes/examples:
Evaluation	Did the student . . . ❑ Offer opinions? ❑ Speculate? ❑ Seek other sources? ❑ Notice omissions? ❑ Analyze arguments?	Notes/examples:

the qualities that they exhibited and note, too, what they did not do. Over time, patterns may emerge, which you might use as a learning objective for future guided instruction.

Misconception analysis. Because misconception analysis is about noticing the thinking students are doing and matching that to correct and incorrect assumptions, anecdotal notes are best for capturing this information. We keep a notebook divided by student name so that we can record our observations as they arise; because it is not always possible to predict when a misconception might occur, we have made a habit of jotting a few notes on these pages at the end of each guided lesson. It's too easy to lose the details in the rush of the day, so our notebooks remind us to take this time.

Conclusion

Guided instruction serves as a linchpin between the focused instruction students have received and the independent learning they will need to complete. The demand on the teacher is high during this phase, particularly because these lessons are subject to quick changes in direction, depending on where the learners lead you. Students are typically grouped with other learners who are similarly performing, based on assessment information, but the groupings change frequently due to ongoing formative assessment. The guided instruction phase can be used to differentiate instruction, as needed, by content, process, or product; the small group size allows for higher levels of customization. The goal of guided instruction is precision teaching that ultimately increases the rate of learning because students do not have to learn again what they already know or try to fill in knowledge gaps on their own. The art and science of teaching come together in this phase, as the teacher responds to the nuances of understanding each student exhibits.

Collaborative Learning: Consolidating Thinking with Peers

In the collaborative learning phase of the gradual release of responsibility instructional framework, students are expected to apply the skills and knowledge they have been taught and to turn to one another for support and enrichment. As they interact with one another, learning moves forward, and students use a number of soft skills—communication, leadership, negotiation—that take on increased importance.

There are a number of different instructional routines used to ensure that students collaborate, but the key is that students assume increased responsibility for their learning and the learning of their peers. The teacher's role shifts to target specific needs through guided instruction.

The Case for Collaborative Learning

Perhaps no element of the gradual release of responsibility instructional framework better captures the essence of college and career readiness than collaborative learning. In fact, the skills students need to work productively in groups are prominently featured in the Common Core State Standards (NGA/CCSSO, 2010a, 2010b):

- The writing standards call for students to actively participate in editing and revision processes with peers. They must collaborate with others to explore print and digital resources to inform their writing.
- The speaking and listening standards ask students to engage with classmates on grade-level topics using recognized methods of discussion, including asking and responding to questions, providing evidence to support claims, reaching consensus, and setting goals and deadlines.
- The mathematics standards require students to justify their conclusions, listen to the reasoning of others, offer counter-examples when needed, and attend to precision in their discussions and explanations in order to make their reasoning clear and understandable to others.

Even in schools unaffected by the Common Core standards, students' ability to communicate and collaborate is rightfully seen as crucial for success. The Partnership for 21st Century Skills calls for students to "exercise flexibility and willingness to be helpful in making necessary compromises to accomplish a common goal" (2009, p. 4). ASCD's Whole Child Initiative's indicators of success for student engagement include opportunities for students to participate in inquiry, decision making, goal setting, self-monitoring, and time management (n.d.). The International Society for Technology in Education states that "digital age skills are vital for preparing students to work, live, and contribute to the social and civic fabric of their communities" and defines communication and collaboration (both face-to-face and at a distance) as one of six major standards for student learning (2012, ¶2).

Teamwork, attitude, and the ability to network and solve problems are collectively referred to as *soft skills* and identified as key to employment opportunities. The U.S. Department of Labor Office of Disability Employment Policy states that "soft skills pay the bills" when it comes to workplace readiness and notes that they "cannot be taught in a vacuum . . . rather, they must be introduced, developed, refined, practiced, and reinforced" (2012, p. 8). Finally, the National Association of Colleges and Employers, an organization dedicated to connecting college students to internships and careers, notes that the soft skills employers most value include leadership, teamwork, verbal communication, and problem solving (2012).

Clearly, problem-solving group skills are essential to college and career readiness, and this is a compelling argument for using collaborative learning. But as educators we also need to pay attention to the "here and now," and that means ensuring our students acquire the academic knowledge of the disciplines we teach. A significant body of evidence suggests that regardless of the subject matter or content area, students learn more and retain information longer when they work in small groups (Dean et al., 2012). Students who work in collaborative groups also appear more satisfied with their classes, complete more assignments, and generally like school better (Summers, 2006).

Collaborative learning is critical in the development of habits of mind necessary within a discipline. Take science, for instance. It is popular for educators to promote "thinking like a scientist" as an overarching goal, but when instruction doesn't match this goal, thinking is undermined. Science students often wrongly believe that the content of their textbooks is set in stone. They don't realize that scientific knowledge evolves precisely because scientists debate findings and engage in discourse meant to expose multiple interpretations (Osborne & Dillon, 2010). Although most of us do not grow up to be scientists in the formal sense, we interact daily with science as members of the public, and "much of what non-scientists need to know in order to make informed judgments about science is knowledge of how science works" (Osborne & Dillon, 2010, p. 22).

Collaborative learning tasks that are structured to provoke debate allow students to engage in true scientific thinking—and we aren't referring strictly to controversial topics in science. In many content areas it's possible to challenge students to examine conflicting quantitative and qualitative data and ask them to draw conclusions and support their claims. That's true scientific thinking.

The Key Features of Collaborative Learning

To understand collaborative learning, it's important to examine its roots in *cooperative learning*. The body of research on cooperative learning, which has informed theory and practice in education for decades, emphasizes the processes that occur within a group, primarily when students are completing a structured task given by the teacher. Here are the five features that define cooperative learning (Johnson, Johnson, & Smith, 1991):

• *Positive interdependence.* The learning situation is interconnected. Each member of the group is important for the overall success of the endeavor.

• *Face-to-face interaction.* Students teach one another, check one another's understanding, discuss concepts and ideas, and make connections between the content and their own lives.

• *Individual and group accountability.* Students understand the products that are expected from the learning task, and they are held accountable for the overall result as well as for their individual contributions.

• *Interpersonal and small-group skills.* All members of working groups possess and use the requisite social skills. Often, specific skills such as leadership, decision making, trust building, turn tak-ing, active listening, and conflict management must be taught.

• *Group processing.* The group members discuss their prog-ress and what they might do to improve their productivity or working relationships.

Implementation of cooperative learning has proven to be problematic for both teachers and students. Teachers cite vari-ance in student goal orientation and skills as a significant bar-rier, often mentioning the student who consistently requests to work alone as an example. Students complain about the lack of accountability in practice, usually recounting a time when they did the lion's share of the work while others did little or nothing. (We rarely hear students tell us they got away with doing nothing, yet they must be out there somewhere.)

Collaborative learning is different from cooperative learning in two important ways. The first is that the task design itself is more broadly defined, and it may be tightly or loosely structured, as in problem-based learning. The second is that the teacher plays an instrumental role in the task. Rather than simply moni-toring group progress and managing the classroom organization, the teacher steps in and out of the group to engage in guided instruction. In other words, whereas the emphasis in cooperative learning is on the social processes used by the group, collabora-tive learning focuses on the cognitive and metacognitive nature of the learning that occurs within the group.

Collaborative learning is also less restricted in terms of learn-ing platforms. Most obviously, it does not insist on face-to-face interaction, as cooperative learning does (Johnson et al., 1991). Because the digital technologies common in classrooms today did not exist when formal descriptions of collaborative learning were taking shape, of course there was no consideration given to social networking and blended learning, both of which allow students to teach one another, check one another's understanding, discuss concepts and ideas, and make connections between the content and their own lives without being in the same place at the same time. Another difference is that collaborative learning does not always feature cooperative learning's group processing, especially when tasks are short and straightforward.

The final aspect of collaborative learning that distinguishes it from cooperative learning is its attention to academic language development: students are encouraged to use the language of the lesson during their interactions with peers. This addition reflects the understanding that humans learn, and think, through language. Students do not become proficient with academic English (or any other language) unless they produce the language. Likewise, simply listening to a proficient user of academic language, such as the teacher, will not ensure that students will develop proficiency in either the language of the discipline or the knowledge of the discipline. Both the vocabulary of the discipline and the units of speech that tie the vocabulary together are important for knowledge acquisition. The academic vocabulary and language of mathematics, for example, has everything to do with understanding mathematics:

> One hallmark of mathematical understanding is the ability to justify, in a way appropriate to the student's mathematical maturity, *why* a particular mathematical statement is true or where a mathematical rule comes from. There is a world of difference between a student who can summon a mnemonic device to expand a product such as $(a + b)(x + y)$ and a student who can explain where the mnemonic comes from. The student who can explain the rule understands the mathematics, and may have a better chance to succeed at a less familiar task such as expanding $(a + b + c)(x + y)$. Mathematical understanding and procedural skill are equally important,

and both are assessable using mathematical tasks of sufficient richness. (NGA/CCSSO, 2010b, p. 4)

In other words, students' use of domain-specific and general academic vocabulary and language is the main way we assess how well they understand concepts and ideas. Without extended opportunities to engage in discourse about their own thinking, students are stunted in their ability to think. This is the shift reflected in the Common Core standards for ELA/literacy and mathematics: teachers are moving from teaching students facts to teaching them to think. Because time does not allow for teachers to engage in extended discourse with each child individually throughout the lesson, there need to be other ways for students to discuss their thinking.

When you boil it down, all collaborative learning has three important features in common: it involves sustained interaction with at least one peer, students use accountable talk in these interactions (Resnick, 1995), and the discourse of the interaction is rooted in the lesson's academic language. However, there is a real difference in the types of tasks students might engage in during collaborative learning. Some tasks are best described as *basic group work,* while other, results-oriented tasks fall into the category of *productive group work.* Both are useful in learning. For teachers, it's simply a matter of considering the purpose the group work is intended to serve. The diagram in Figure 4.1 compares and contrasts these two forms of collaborative learning, which we'll take a closer look at now.

Basic Group Work: For Sharing Information and Exchanging Ideas

In basic group work, the students share their own ideas, values, or beliefs and consider those of others. These sharing activities

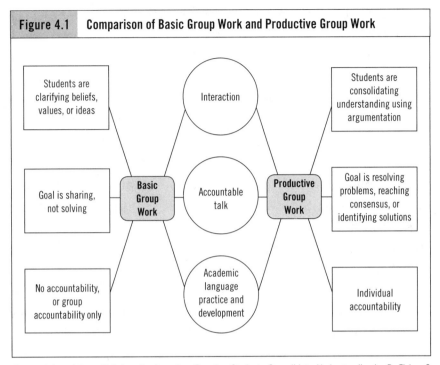

Figure 4.1   Comparison of Basic Group Work and Productive Group Work

Students are clarifying beliefs, values, or ideas

Interaction

Students are consolidating understanding using argumentation

Goal is sharing, not solving

Basic Group Work

Accountable talk

Productive Group Work

Goal is resolving problems, reaching consensus, or identifying solutions

No accountability, or group accountability only

Academic language practice and development

Individual accountability

Source: Adapted from *Collaborative Learning: Ensuring Students Consolidate Understanding* by D. Fisher & N. Frey. Copyright 2012 by the International Reading Association.

are the most common kind of group work we see. A good example is the classic "think-pair-share" arrangement and its many variations, such as think-write-pair-share and think-pair-square (where two pairs join together to extend their discussion), which we've seen used in nearly every classroom we've ever been in. These sharing tasks tend to be brief, and many are deployed on the fly for purposes of engagement and classroom management, especially when students indicate that attention is beginning to wander.

Other basic group work is more extended and purposeful. For example, Art Hollingsworth, a Family and Human Services teacher in his district's Career and Technical Education pathway, uses *opinion stations* to provoke discussion about beliefs and values in one of his units. Here's how he explains his approach:

I teach about mandatory reporting requirements for the profession, but I'm also working with adolescents who have a very different set of beliefs about privacy. They value keeping secrets because they've learned that it's important in friendships. I need them to see that mandatory reporting of suspected abuse and neglect among clients is not the same as keeping a harmless secret between two friends.

Mr. Hollingsworth has large signs in each of the four corners of his classroom: Strongly Agree, Agree, Disagree, and Strongly Disagree. ("I don't use Neutral, because it forces them to take a stand," he told us.) After he reads aloud brief scenarios of Family and Human Services personnel being confronted with evidence of possible abuse or neglect, and their decision on whether to report it to a state agency, students then move to the corner that best fits their opinion regarding the decision, and they discuss it with their peers. "One scenario in particular gets them stirred up," Mr. Hollingsworth said. "I give them a case of a child care worker who repeatedly sees bruises on a child, with the mom explaining it away as a clumsy child." Many of his students want to debate the child care worker's decision to file a report, claiming that she didn't have evidence. "This really pushes their thinking, and we go back into the language of the mandatory reporting law, which states that they don't need to investigate, only to suspect." His goal—for students to clarify their values and beliefs—paves the way for more instruction.

Another way to incorporate a planned exchange of ideas is to use a *carousel* arrangement, in which groups of students rotate through a series of stations, gathering information (often background knowledge) for the purpose of discussion. Third grade teacher Emily Aldrich uses a carousel as part of a science unit on properties of light. Students visit a station that features a prism (so they can learn about refraction), another on shadows (to see how sources of light alter the shapes of the shadows), and a third featuring compact discs. In this last station, students experiment with locating different light sources such as the natural light of the sun coming through the classroom windows, tilting the CDs just so to find the rainbow reflection. At each station, they discuss and record their observations.

Ms. Aldrich told us how using the carousel arrangement supports her instructional goals:

> This is my introduction to a unit [on light], and I want them to grasp two concepts right away. The first is that I want them to notice that when you change the position of the light source relative to an object, the shadow it casts changes as well. The second is that visible light refracts into a rainbow of colors. Later, we'll be looking at how the reflection and absorption of visible light dictates the perceived color of an object. I'll use their observations as a springboard.

Ms. Aldrich's use of basic group work is an example of how collaborative learning can be used in an inquiry-based classroom. As we have noted, there is a misconception that the gradual release of responsibility instructional framework requires that every lesson proceed through a strict sequence, with collaborative learning always following focused or guided instruction. But many classrooms, especially science ones, regularly use inquiry to foster curiosity, activate background knowledge, and set the stage for new learning. By opening the unit with collaborative learning, Ms. Aldrich is tapping into the concepts, knowledge, and skills her students already possess as they write and discuss their observations. She is not introducing new knowledge; she is asking students to apply their existing knowledge to a novel situation. Her goal is consistent with the goals of basic group work, in that she wants her students to share ideas but not yet resolve problems or identify solutions. For that, she will choose a productive group work arrangement.

Guided Instruction During Basic Group Work

One common instructional arrangement, especially in the elementary grades, is to devote part of a lesson to centers or stations. This has particular merit in that it teaches young students to work independently and encourages their communication and collaboration skills as they work with their classmates. While students are engaged in this work, the teacher is able to meet with other needs-based groups of students for guided instruction. For this reason, centers or stations are primarily designed to provide practice opportunities for students as they approach mastery of a skill or concept. Therefore, the tasks students are completing are on the lower end of complexity so that the collaborative group can function with a minimum amount of teacher supervision or input.

However, students won't simply begin working effectively at centers or stations just because a teacher told them to. They must be taught how to begin the work and function as a group. The logistics of the centers—including signals, locating materials, and turning in assignments— should be clear to students. We strongly encourage elementary teachers to devote the first four weeks (20 days) of school to systematically introducing and practicing the stations they plan to use often. Begin by teaching the entire class the processes of one center and allowing time for practice. A few days later, introduce a second center in the same way. Once students are comfortable with the second center, divide the class in half and have each half complete first one center and then the other. Repeat this pattern as you introduce new centers, further subdividing the class until you have all of the centers up and running. Once these processes are smooth, you will be able to devote time to meeting with needs-based groups for guided instruction. Figure 4.2 presents a 20-day calendar for systematically phasing in basic group work centers or stations.

Figure 4.2	20-Day Plan for Implementing Basic Group Work Centers			
Day 1	**Day 2**	**Day 3**	**Day 4**	**Day 5**
Collaborative learning lesson *What are the goals and expectations of group learning?*	Introduce Station 1	Practice, circulate, and evaluate Station 1 Observe students and evaluate procedures	Introduce Station 2	Practice, circulate, and evaluate Station 2 Observe students and evaluate procedures
Day 6	**Day 7**	**Day 8**	**Day 9**	**Day 10**
Implement Stations 1 and 2 Divide class in half; switch	Collaborative learning lesson *How do you get help when your group is stuck?*	Introduce Station 3	Practice, circulate, and evaluate Station 3 Observe students and evaluate procedures	Implement Stations 1, 2, 3 Introduce schedule; complete three rotations
Day 11	**Day 12**	**Day 13**	**Day 14**	**Day 15**
Assessment Implement Stations 1, 2, 3; assess individuals or small groups	Collaborative learning lesson *How do you offer, accept, decline, and ask for help?*	Introduce Station 4	Practice, circulate, and evaluate Station 4 Observe students and evaluate procedures	Implement Stations 1–4 Introduce schedule; complete three rotations
Day 16	**Day 17**	**Day 18**	**Day 19**	**Day 20**
Assessment Implement Stations 1–4; assess individuals or small groups	Introduce Station 5	Practice, circulate, and evaluate Station 5 Observe students and evaluate procedures	Collaborative learning lesson *How do you know you are finished? What do you do next?*	Introduce teacher-directed station with five collaborative stations

Source: From *Productive Group Work: How to Engage Students, Build Teamwork, and Promote Understanding,* by N. Frey, D. Fisher, & S. Everlove. Copyright 2009 by ASCD.

Productive Group Work: For Solving Problems and Finding Solutions

Basic group work is valuable because it allows students to express their ideas, values, and beliefs, and it gives them an opportunity to apply listening and speaking skills as they engage with classmates. But basic group work primarily draws on existing knowledge.

A crucial aspect of the gradual release of responsibility instructional framework is that students encounter problems that require them to consolidate and advance their thinking, using newer knowledge in order to reach resolution. This goal is markedly different from those associated with basic group work, and it is the hallmark of productive group work. In productive group work, there is always a product, accountability is at the group and the individual levels, and students use argumentation—especially furnishing evidence—to support their conclusions.

Solving problems and identifying solutions are central thinking goals in productive group work. This means students must apply the soft skills related to timekeeping, goal setting, and making work plans for the group. These can be especially challenging for young students, who will benefit from scaffolding—supports such as language frames that provide a structure for their discussions, note-taking sheets designed to capture the group's ideas, and checklists for tasks that require multiple meetings, such as those that involve research and presentation of ideas.

Four Productive Group Work Routines Every Student Should Know

There are many well-known instructional routines that can be utilized for productive group work. We have four favorites—techniques that are not discipline-specific and are easily transferable to varied subject matter. In fact, we encourage teachers who share students—co-teachers or members of a grade-level team, especially—to teach these four routines so that they can be easily enacted across content areas.

Discussion Roundtable

We were inspired by the work of English teacher and author Jim Burke (2002) to adapt the technique he calls *conversational roundtable* to promote discussion and note taking within productive work groups. We ask students to fold a sheet of paper into fourths and then fold down the interior corner in order to create a diamond in the center of the opened page (see Figure 4.3). Students make their own notes in the upper left quadrant of the graphic organizer and then explain their thinking to the rest of the group. Members of the group record notes about one another's ideas and then write a summary or conclusion in the center. The group submits its graphic organizers to the teacher, who now has a record of how the conversation evolved, what each person's contributions were to the discussion, and the more advanced thinking that occurred for each individual after the discussion.

We have seen this customized in other content areas. In mathematics, groups are assigned a complex word problem, and each contributor is responsible for proposing a different element to solving the problem. One student determines what the problem is asking them to solve, another creates a visual representation, another calculates the problem, and the fourth links it to a math model. After the discussion, the students independently write a justification for their solution.

Collaborative Posters

Working with their peers to create visual displays helps make students' connections between ideas and information transparent. Pam Tran uses a collaborative poster (a form of visual display)

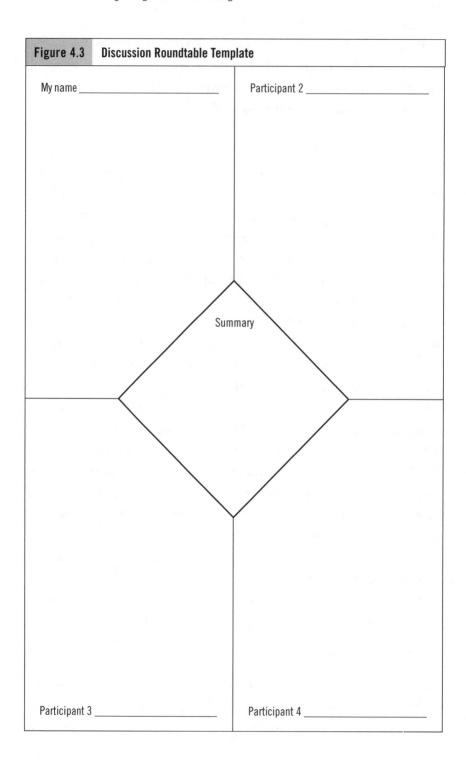

Figure 4.3   Discussion Roundtable Template

My name _____   Participant 2 _____

Summary

Participant 3 _____   Participant 4 _____

with her geometry students to teach them the process of proofs. Each group of four students is given a different task, or proof, to solve. Each member of the group has a different-colored marker and is required to sign his or her name on the back of the poster. This ensures that each student contributes to the poster and is accountable for the information on the poster. During their discussions, students apply what they have learned about proofs during focus lessons and guided instruction, including the process Ms. Tran has modeled for them several times:

1. Identify or generate the statement of the theorem.
2. State the given.
3. Create a drawing that represents the given.
4. State what you're going to prove.
5. Provide the proof.

The modeling of this process of solving proofs is critical, and the guided instruction students receive can be used to correct misconceptions and address knowledge gaps; the collaborative learning task requires students to use what they know.

Collaborative posters can be used for different grades and subject areas. For example, a group of 1st graders might create a Venn diagram to identify the similarities and differences between two characters, a group of 6th graders might use a timeline to aid their understanding of the various kingdoms and dynasties in Egyptian history, and a group of biology students could demonstrate their understanding of cell division by creating a process chart.

Reciprocal Teaching

Reciprocal teaching is an instructional strategy in which groups of four students read a piece of text and then engage in a conversation about the text (Palinscar & Brown, 1984). The conversation is structured around four strategies: summarizing, question generating, clarifying, and predicting. As with most collaborative structures, students need practice and modeling before they can use reciprocal teaching with their peers. The approach is most effective when students understand the four comprehension strategies that comprise the conversation (Oczkus, 2010).

Summarizing is a brief written or oral review of the main points of the text. Text can be summarized across sentences, paragraphs, or the selection as a whole. When students first use reciprocal teaching, they typically focus on sentence- and paragraph-level summaries. As they become skilled with procedures, they begin to summarize at the paragraph and passage levels.

Questioning focuses students on inquiry and investigation. As students generate questions, they identify the type of information that is important enough to provide the basis for a question. During the questioning portion of a reciprocal teaching discussion, students often answer one another's questions and thus engage in conversations that extend beyond the text. Over time, and with modeling and practice, students learn to generate questions at many levels of complexity. For example, students might learn to ask the four types of questions common in question–answer relationships (i.e., right there, think and search, author and you, on your own; Raphael, Highfield, & Au, 2006), or they might focus on text-dependent questions such as key details, vocabulary and text structure, author's purpose, inferences, or opinions and arguments (Fisher & Frey, 2013).

Clarifying is a metacognitive activity in which students learn to notice things that they don't understand. During the discussion about the text, students ask for clarification on components of the text that blocked their comprehension. Early in the use of reciprocal teaching, students often seek clarification on individual words. Over time, students will also clarify ideas that confuse them, missing background information that others might have, and unfamiliar experiences discussed in the text. In addition, with modeling and practice, students can incorporate another comprehension strategy, visualizing, into their clarifying. One of the ways to teach readers this strategy is to tell them to "make a movie in your mind" as they read.

Predicting is the process of making an educated guess, based on the best information available, about what might happen next. In order to make predictions successfully, students must activate both background and prior knowledge, pay attention to what the author has said, and make inferences. Predicting also keeps readers engaged with the text, as they want to read further to determine if their predictions are correct.

For an example of how reciprocal teaching can help students advance toward independent learning, consider what went on in Tony Nelson's 4th grade science class during a unit focused on nutrition, exercise, and fitness. Following a series of focus lessons and guided instructional events, students were ready to work in collaborative groups. Each productive work group had copies of the "Choose My Plate" informational poster produced by the U.S. Department of Agriculture (see www.choosemyplate.gov/). They used summarizing, clarifying, questioning, and predicting to read and discuss this text, and the members of each group developed their own notes regarding each of these elements of reciprocal teaching. This text generated more questions for the groups than anything else in the unit. As an extension, Mr. Nelson asked his students to select one of their group's questions for further research. Angel's group identified a number of them for further inquiry:

- What is a healthy food item? An unhealthy food item?
- Why is it important that we eat healthfully?
- How many food items did we eat last night that were considered healthy? Unhealthy?
- Do you think you are eating healthy meals according to the diagram?

- What might you want to change to eat better?
- Is it possible to eat better at home? At school?

Angel selected the final question and began her quest for the answer through Internet searches and additional print and digital readings, looking for possible answers. Over the weeklong investigation of their questions, students drafted responses, met with Mr. Nelson for editing sessions, met with peers for feedback, and read extensively. Angel's answer was complex and read, in part, like this:

> It is possible to eat better, if you want to and if adults help. With some education, parents and cafeteria staff could prepare very healthy meals. This would mean that students would have to stop begging for unhealthy meals, like fried food. To eat healthier, students need choices and they need to make good choices.

In the case of Mr. Nelson's lesson, all the students were reading and commenting on the same piece of text. There are other times, however, when you want students to consolidate their understanding across multiple documents or artifacts. To accomplish this, use a jigsaw arrangement to promote synthesis of knowledge.

Jigsaw

In this collaborative learning routine, each group member learns some unique material and then teaches it to other group members. Elliot Aronson developed the jigsaw classroom in 1971 in Austin, Texas, in response to the kind of in-class conflict he was seeing (see www.jigsaw.org). In most classrooms at the time, students competed against each another for grades and had few opportunities and little motivation to collaborate. Aronson's goal was to restructure the classroom for positive interdependence.

Although Aronson's original work was conducted in a 5th grade classroom, this approach can be used across grade levels and content areas. History teacher Javier Vaca routinely uses the jigsaw method when students are learning about primary and secondary source materials. In their home groups, students gain knowledge about individual documents and then share this knowledge with the other members of their group. But each student is also a member of an expert group, where students jointly build their expertise about a particular document. The expert group is key to making jigsaw work, as individuals benefit from the collective wisdom of the group. This also ensures that a group is not inadvertently left behind due to the fact that an individual assigned to a document did not understand it.

During a unit on the American home front war effort during World War II, Cassandra worked within an expert group of students assigned to analyze the text from Franklin Delano Roosevelt's 20th fireside chat from February 23, 1942, "On the Progress of the War." Cassandra's group chunked the long text and used a reciprocal teaching approach to discuss it in depth. Lex, a member of the expert group, commented on FDR's opening allusion to Washington's troops at Valley Forge; the group consulted a map in order to better understand troop movements and critical territories. Cassandra drew their attention back to the end of the radio broadcast text, noting that the president was beseeching his listeners to focus their efforts on increasing military supply production and set aside labor disputes in order to meet demand.

Forty-five minutes later, Cassandra rejoined her home group, made up of students who had become experts on other documents. During the remainder of this class period as well as the following day, she and her home group members taught one another about the war bond effort and viewed several film clips used in movie theater campaigns. They read a secondary source describing the rationing program for civilians and viewed images of rationing coupons. One student in their home group, Mario, taught them about the victory garden program promoted as a means for Americans to supplement their rationed canned goods. He noted that he had learned that victory gardens were not confined to the American war effort and that many countries had promoted their use as far back as World War I. "I think it's interesting that they coupled this with rationing and made sure that people knew their sacrifices were to support the war effort," he said. After everyone's presentations, the group moved to a synthesis of these documents. The conclusions they drew included the fact that these efforts were necessary from an economic standpoint but were strategically presented to the American people as a way to actively contribute to a cause. As Cassandra explained to Mr. Vaca,

> A lot of times people think that individually they don't make much of a difference. It seems like the government placed a lot of effort in getting people involved and keeping them up to date on what was happening. When you're involved, you feel like you can make a sacrifice for the greater good and that it will mean something.

Specialized Routines for Productive Group Work

In addition to these generic productive group work routines, there are a number of specialized routines that teachers can use to engage students in learning. We will consider two such routines, both of which provide students an enhanced opportunity to interact with one another and the content.

Literature Circles and Book Clubs

Literature circles (Daniels, 2001) and book clubs (McMahon, Raphael, Goatley, & Pardo, 2007) have been popular approaches for differentiating texts among readers because they allow for peer-led, small-group discussions of a common text. Students do not read in the presence of others (this is done during independent reading or at home); they gather together to discuss what they have read. The literature circles approach stresses choice and the temporary nature of the groups, as configurations change with the next round of books. Several principles are central to literature circles:

• *Students have choice in the books they read.* These choices are often limited to a list the teacher has compiled (usually chosen because they have a common theme and represent a range of text complexity), but students choose which they will read, sometimes with some "artful teacher guidance" (Daniels, 2006, p. 11). Group formation is then predicated on book choice, which really creates an interest group.

• *Students have a responsibility to themselves and to their peers.* These responsibilities include record keeping, contributing to group discussions, and, of course, keeping up with the assignment. It is hard to hide in a group of six or so when you have not done the reading! Students create their own ground rules and schedule the times they will meet. Once comfortable with the process, groups jointly determine how much they will read before the next meeting.

• *There is increased engagement in these peer-led discussions.* Daniels calls this "airtime," and it stands to reason that in a small group the level of participation is going to increase (2006, p. 11). Drawing a quiet student into the discussion becomes the job of supportive peers, not the teacher.

The social development of these groups can be challenging for some students, who may have come to rely on teacher-directed instruction to the exclusion of any responsibility for their own learning. Many teachers initially use role sheets to formalize the necessary social and academic behaviors necessary for effective peer-led discussions. These roles typically align with the content of the discussion, such as Discussion Director, Vocabulary Enricher, and so on. Once students become adept at literature circle discussion, these formal roles are abandoned in favor of a more natural ebb and flow to the conversation.

Now, an illustration. Arneta Johnson's 5th grade students have been participating in literature circles since the beginning of the school year, and they are now in their fourth cycle. Each cycle features a unifying essential question to be answered through whole-class shared reading as collaborative groups read one of five literature club titles. The essential question for this cycle is, "Why do some people act bravely in the face of danger, while others do not?" Ms. Johnson is reading Anne Frank's diary (1953), a complex text, with the entire class. The students, as part of their literature circles, are also reading one of the following:

- *Sacajawea* (Bruchac, 2001),
- *Stealing Home: The Story of Jackie Robinson* (Denenberg, 1990),
- *Chief: The Life of Peter J. Ganci, a New York City Firefighter* (Ganci, 2003),
- *Harvesting Hope: The Story of Cesar Chavez* (Krull, 2003), and
- *Voices from the Fields: Children of Migrant Farmworkers Tell Their Stories* (Atkin, 2000).

Ms. Johnson selected these books carefully to represent a range of possible answers to the question, including righting an injustice, saving the lives of others, and venturing into new realms. She considered gender, ethnicity, and age, as well as text difficulty (two of the selections are picture books). She previewed each title during a book talk, and students made their top three selections. This allowed her to shape the groups so that they were equally distributed and to match a few students with books that were not significantly above their reading level.

For two weeks, literature circles met to discuss the readings and then recorded their reactions in their reading journals. Jessica's group read *Harvesting Hope;* they ended each discussion by revisiting the essential question to see if they had developed an answer. At the end of the two weeks, each student wrote an essay about the question, using examples from their literature circle selection and *Anne Frank.* Jessica's essay contained the following paragraph:

> I think people are brave and not brave for lots of reasons. Anne was brave because she felt like she had to be to survive. She wasn't a sad girl and she stayed brave on the outside even when she was scared on the inside. She knew it made it easier for her family, too. Cesar Chavez was brave for a different reason. He knew what was happening was wrong. He didn't like seeing so many people he cared about being treated that way. So he stood up for everyone. Maybe Anne and Cesar had one thing in common about being brave. They both cared about other people.

Labs and Simulations

Labs and simulations are an ideal structure for collaborative learning because they allow for student interaction and inquiry. Labs are most common in science education, but they can also be used in art and physical education. In science classrooms, students should "participate in a range of lab activities to verify known scientific concepts, pose research questions, conceive their own investigations, and create models of natural phenomena" (Singer, Hilton, & Schweingruber, 2006). Participating in these types of activities, especially within a gradual release of responsibility instructional framework, helps students understand the content.

Consider the following example, from Justin Miller's science class, of students applying what they have learned about electricity in a science lab. In their lab groups, students were given several fruits and vegetables (lemons, potatoes, grapefruit, tomatoes, and oranges), shiny copper pennies, zinc-plated screws, wires with alligator clips, a light-emitting diode (LED) with a low voltage rating, and a multimeter. Their collaborative task was to consolidate the knowledge gained thus far and to light the LED. Once groups had successfully delivered electricity to the LED, they used the multimeter to measure the amount of electricity produced. Thus, the task was twofold: first, use the supplies to make electricity and then, second, determine which arrangement produced the most electricity. Each student had to form a hypothesis and then work with the group to test it.

Mr. Miller did not simply walk around the room to manage this lab. He knew that this was the ideal time for him to provide guided instruction and push students' thinking to higher levels. He first met with a group of four students whose formative assessment results had indicated they were struggling to grasp the concepts of circuits and conductors. With them, he shared the Eyewitness book *Electricity* (Parker, 2005), particularly the illustration on page 22 providing a visual explanation of circuits and conductors.

Nearby, one of the groups had inserted a penny in one side of the lemon and a zinc-plated screw into the other. They connected the wires to the penny and screw and then lit the LED. Mr. Miller looked up and asked the members of the group if they could make their signal strength any stronger. He also reminded them that they each had to explain, in their science journals, why this worked; Andrew noted in his journal that "when the screw contacted with the citric acid in the lemon, it started two chemical reactions: oxidation and reduction."

Like labs, simulations are used to ensure that learning is applied (Aldrich, 2005). Simulations are common in social studies, language arts, and other content areas for learning such things as cause and effect. Simulations International (www.simulationsintl.

com), a global company that provides simulation consulting, identified five elements of simulations. If these elements are present, the activity qualifies as a simulation:

- The simulation itself is not real but aims to mimic reality.
- The simulation contains a mathematical or rules-based model.
- Time is continuous.
- Where you are is always a consequence of what you have done in the past.
- Where you are going is completely your choice.

In her government class, Janice Fink uses simulations of town hall meetings and congressional voting. During one session, she provided students with a scenario very real to their lives: drag racing on the freeway. She distributed copies of a newspaper article about drag racing, a political cartoon on the subject, a section of the vehicle code, and a proposed amendment to the code, which would criminalize observing drag racing. The room was charged, and students began sharing their opinions about this with one another. Ms. Fink interrupted their conversations and reminded them of the process of a town hall meeting.

She assigned her students roles as mayor, council members, community members, parents of a young adult killed while drag racing, business owners, observers of drag races, three well-known drag racers, and police officers. Ms. Fink reminded her students that the conversation could go in any direction they chose, as long as they respected the town hall process and remained in their roles. In their collaborative groups, students shared their thinking about the proposed law and provided feedback and commentary.

During this time, Ms. Fink met with individual students who needed additional support to make their position known. She also met with the mayor and council members in a small guided instruction group to remind them of their role in the discussion and how to manage the town hall meeting. Over several days, with focus lessons, guided instruction, and collaborative learning events, the students were prepared for the simulation.

Janae started the conversation:

> Mr. Mayor and Members of the Council: I can't believe that you're thinking of making it a crime to watch drag racing. What could I, the observer, do? Where will it stop? Will it be a crime to observe a house robbery? Will it be a crime to watch someone run a stop sign or light? And who will enforce this rule?

Marvin asked to speak next. His role was "business owner":

> I like drag racing, so it doesn't matter what rules you make up.

Ms. Fink interrupted the group and reminded students that they had to be true to their role. To Marvin, she said, "Which business owner's perspective are you speaking from? Think about that. Some business owners might sympathize with what you just said, but others would disagree with you. Maybe you should start over and introduce yourself. That would give us the context for your speech."

Over the course of the town hall meeting, many different opinions were expressed, ideas were challenged, and positions were forwarded. Ms. Fink knew that her students were ready for this simulation because of the structure of her classroom and the work she had done to prepare them.

Guided Instruction During Productive Group Work

Gathering formative assessment data to inform instruction means that the teacher is actively involved in productive group work. The most common form of involvement is when teachers insert themselves into group discussions for the purpose of checking for understanding. When a group appears stuck or has only a partial understanding of a concept, the teacher momentarily assumes cognitive responsibility and moves through the same instructional moves described in Chapter 3's look at guided instruction. Teachers can follow questions with prompts that cause students to activate their background knowledge, recall a procedure or prompt, or utilize an informal problem-solving heuristic they have applied in the past.

The task complexity is elevated in productive group work because you want to provoke errors. That's right: you want students to make mistakes, because mistakes lead to learning. In cognitive science, this is called *productive failure* (Kapur, 2008). It requires a shift in the teacher's role to provide shorter guided instruction as part of the process of gathering formative assessment information. The teacher travels from group to group to listen in, check for understanding, and help groups get "unstuck" when their understanding breaks down and they have run out of solutions.

To be sure, these visits should be delicately timed; you don't want to swoop in too early and thwart the group's problem-solving process as they figure out what to do next. However, most of us have witnessed the group that has ground to a halt. When that occurs, you temporarily take back cognitive responsibility, asking questions and providing prompts regarding background knowledge, previously learned procedures, and informal heuristics. Keep in mind that groups in this phase often temporarily forget previously learned skills and concepts because they are not yet expert at doing what experts can: recognizing patterns, envisioning next steps, and seeing concepts as schemata, rather than random points of information (Bransford, Brown, & Cocking, 2000). In this case, the guided instruction moves the group forward again, now with a more complete understanding than they possessed at the beginning of the task.

Formative Assessment During Collaborative Learning

Checking for understanding is essential at each phase of the gradual release of responsibility model (Fisher & Frey, 2007a). This can seem to be more of a challenge in collaborative learning because so much of the activity is taking place outside the teacher's presence. Yet the key to gathering formative assessment information is to design individual accountability within productive group work tasks. The students in Mr. Nelson's class chose a question for further research and produced a report. Ms. Tran's geometry students developed a collaborative poster using a format that allowed her to determine the level of participation for each member.

These are the guiding questions we use to design formative assessment tasks for collaborative learning (Frey & Fisher, 2011):

- What evidence do I need in order to make future instructional decisions?
- What evidence would be most useful for guided instruction follow-up?
- Does this assessment task provide meaningful feedback to the student?
- Can every member of the group do this assessment task in a meaningful way?
- If not, in what ways can this assessment task be modified to meet the needs of those students?

Sometimes during productive group work, students will temporarily forget what they already know because they are focused on the newer information they are attempting to apply. Novices are not the best at noticing patterns and marshaling resources to resolve problems. That's precisely what you're looking for during productive group work because the goal is for them to consolidate their understanding. When you notice that students need to remember what they know, you shift back to guided instruction.

Conclusion

Collaborative learning provides a critical bridge in student learning because it allows novice learners to refine their thinking about new concepts and skills. The oral language development in such settings is particularly valuable because it requires the use of social and academic language in order to accomplish the task. Individual accountability is a hallmark of productive group work as it minimizes the frustration felt by some students who believe they have shouldered an unfair burden. The configuration of the group is important to its success. Although there are times when student choice or interest groups are useful, in most cases the grouping should be heterogeneous so as not to impoverish some groups that have fewer collective resources among them. This is just as important for high-achieving students, who tend to collaborate less in groups they perceive as needing less of their help.

5

Independent Learning: Applying What Has Been Taught

All learning is "independent" in the sense that the learner's motivation, interest, and ability to learn mark the difference between success and failure. Even during the focused instruction phase, when the cognitive responsibility lies primarily with the teacher, the learner is a partner in the process. As the cognitive load increases for the student, the need for self-direction grows. Therefore, the independent learning phase is merely the fullest expression of the skills and habits of mind used throughout the entire gradual release of responsibility instructional framework. As we have noted previously, it is important for students to consolidate their understanding with peers during collaborative learning. In this chapter, we focus on the role of application. Application requires deliberate practice: time spent working and thinking alone. As Ericsson, Krampe, and Tesch-Rober (1993) note, serious study alone, what they call *solitary practice,* is one of the strongest predictors of expert performance. Like Ericsson and colleagues, Gladwell (2008) acknowledges that it takes about 10,000 hours of deliberate practice to develop expertise. This has significant implications for teachers and school, in terms of developing students' content knowledge.

A common misconception about independent learning is that the ultimate goal is for the student to replicate what has been taught. But independent learning is far more complex than that. The process of figuring things out, which begins during focused instruction, continues. Struggle is essential for learning; expecting that students should somehow be "perfect" by the time they reach the independent learning phase isn't setting the bar high enough. In Chapter 4, we discussed productive failure (Kapur, 2008), and this process of learning from mistakes continues during independent learning. Duke (2012) illustrates this point while recounting a music teacher's experience:

> A student in her class was trying to figure out a piano fingering as she was standing beside him watching. After several unsuccessful repetitions, he looked to her and said, "If you were a good teacher, you'd tell me how to do this," whereupon my very astute and skillful grad student replied, "Yes, but because I'm an excellent teacher, I'm going to wait a while longer while you figure it out." Of course, she said that with the informed confidence that her student could in fact figure it out, which he did after the next few attempts. Think about what the student learned from that experience, other than the fact that his teacher's a hard nose. He discovered that he could figure it out. His moments in the muddle led to his arriving at an advantageous solution, and all of the errors he made along the way actually strengthened the memory of the solution and the path he took in reaching it. (p. 40)

Duke's story captures an important element of independent learning, and that is that the music teacher was sure that the student's previous learning had properly equipped him to succeed.

In this chapter, we will examine what independent learning is and describe the conditions and skills necessary to implement it effectively. First, we'll look at the need to teach students how to learn through the development of metacognition and self-regulation. Then we will consider independent learning tasks, both in school and outside it, paying special attention to homework and blended learning practices. Finally, we will examine the crucial role of the teacher during independent learning. It's more than just assigning work, and formative assessment is key.

Key Features of Independent Learning

We've heard it a thousand times: "All children can learn." In truth, that maxim describes only part of the formula for what propels independent learning. Of course all students have the capacity to learn. But what about the *ability* to learn? Ability is built on skill, and students need to be taught how to think about their own thinking (*metacognition*) and how to act upon their learning (*self-regulation*).

Metacognition

The onset of an awareness of one's own thinking coincides with the age of formal schooling (4 years old or so), but this awareness must be purposefully nurtured over a child's academic career. Metacognition is the learner's mindful acknowledgment of his or her own learning processes, the conditions under which one learns best, and a recognition that learning has occurred (Flavell, 1979). This is truly a lifelong phenomenon and, therefore, not something that can be taught in a handful of lessons; teachers must return to the topic again and again.

The gradual release of responsibility instructional framework supports the development of metacognition in that students are provided with time to recognize that learning has occurred and under what conditions. Work to build this awareness begins during focused instruction, as the teacher thinks aloud (calling attention to the decision-making process), and it extends through guided instruction as the teacher prompts students to notice what they know and do not know. Students assume more responsibility for their metacognition as they explain their thinking, justify solutions, and listen to the thinking of others in collaborative learning groups.

The goal is for students to independently work to understand their thinking process. Anderson (2002) suggests a series of four questions that challenge learners to move from cognition to metacognition. Teachers can post these questions on the board at the beginning of the lesson and write the answers as the class moves through a lesson or activity. Metacognitive self-talk can be fostered by encouraging students to use these four questions during both collaborative and independent learning:

1. *"What am I trying to accomplish?"* This first question aims to move learners from merely copying a task to identifying that task's intended outcomes. ("This math word problem is asking me to figure out how many people can be served with the number of apple pies at the picnic.")

2. *"What strategies am I using?"* After identifying the problem and the goal, the next step is to figure out what strategies can be used to achieve a solution. ("I really need to use two strategies to find the answer. First I have to multiply the number of slices by the total number of pies. That will give me the total number of servings. But then I also have to divide those servings among the people at the picnic.")

3. *"How well am I using the strategies?"* Once again, monitoring plays an important role in the acquisition of new learning. This question reminds students that effective use of a skill or strategy comes from pausing from time to time during the process to see

how well it's working. ("Before I divide, I need to check to see if what I've multiplied makes sense. Could it be that 8 apple pies could be cut into a total of 64 slices? I also want to check my math. Does $8 \times 8 = 64$?")

4. *"What else could I do?"* The goal of this question is to teach students to think flexibly and avoid getting bogged down in rigid thinking. At this stage of learning, it is common for students to focus on new skills and strategies and temporarily forget previously learned skills and strategies they have at their disposal. By asking "What else could I do?" they remind themselves that those familiar strategies could play a role. ("I'm still not sure I am doing this correctly. One way I can be sure is if I draw a diagram of the pies and the people. We've done diagramming before when we've had tough word problems. I'm going to try that now.")

Whether in mathematics or any other content area, students need to see how to prepare and plan, select an approach, and monitor the execution of their plan (Anderson, 2002). This is especially valuable during independent learning, when students are driving their own progress. Persistence is vital as well, and students who have a metacognitive process can think their way through a difficult patch, get themselves unstuck, and figure it out for themselves.

Self-Regulation

All students need to self-regulate as they engage in independent learning. Self-regulation includes acting upon the metacognitive perceptions they experience during a task, such as rereading a passage when comprehension breaks down, consulting another resource to clarify the meaning of a vaguely understood vocabulary term, or checking one's work for errors after completion. These metacognitive behaviors are linked to the learner's intentions and goals, such as finishing the task, doing it well, and receiving positive feedback. In other words, metacognitive awareness is the starting point. The behaviors that follow it constitute a learner's regulation.

Time management. Checklists and reminders to use problem-solving questions, like the four we have just looked at, are a significant way to scaffold students' developing ability to self-regulate. Many teachers build regulatory supports into longer independent learning projects. For example, a 3rd grade teacher may require a daily check-in to gauge progress on a science research report. Young children have difficulty managing time, and these interim checkpoints can be of great help to them.

Task prioritization. Another aspect of self-regulation is prioritizing tasks. Younger students are not especially good at determining which tasks are more difficult and therefore require more attention. Dufresne and Kobisagawa (1989) presented a range of paired words for students in grades 1 through 7 to memorize and then gave them time to study. The students in the lower grades did not know how to allocate their time to focus on the more difficult items to memorize, which is what the 5th through 7th grade students did. Teachers can support the development of this self-regulatory process by providing directions that identify the more difficult and time-consuming elements of an assignment.

Calibration. A third component of self-regulation during independent learning is *calibration,* the ability to accurately self-assess in order to affect learning decisions. Calibration is a newer area of research in metacognition and self-regulation, and it focuses primarily on students' knowledge of the gap between where their current performance is and what they hope to achieve (Hattie, 2013). A meta-analysis conducted by Hattie (2009) found that self-reported expectations and self-grading are among the most effective instructional approaches a teacher can use. For example, students in general can accurately predict their score on a test, although this ability declines among students who perform poorly. Why is this? Hattie notes that students who possess inaccurate information are more likely to be overconfident—in other words, they don't know what they don't know. Therefore, they are less able to effectively allocate attention to items in need of further consideration. This inability to calibrate extends to teachers as well. In one series of large-scale studies, elementary teachers underestimated task difficulty by one grade level, whereas high school teachers overestimated task difficulty by one grade level (Hattie, Brown, & Keegan, 2005).

The vision of a roomful of students silently toiling away on an assignment while the teacher spends the entire time filing papers and putting materials away is wrongheaded. Independent learning, when it occurs in the classroom, should include metacognitive supports that encourage growth in self-regulation. The teacher provides this support through feedback on the tasks students complete inside and outside the classroom.

Independent Learning Inside School

There is a wide range of independent learning tasks that students can complete during school, including journal and essay writing; independent reading; designing and drafting projects and performances; preparing for discussions, debates, and seminars; quizzes and other assessments; and research. These tasks should allow for students to demonstrate their understanding of the content, *not* replicate the work the teacher has done. It is also critical that independent tasks students complete during school are not simply low-level assignments that require them to do little but regurgitate what they already know.

The Literacy Design Collaborative (www.literacydesign-collaborative.org) has developed useful sets of task templates that encourage students to continue to build knowledge during independent learning. The templates are organized by the critical thinking skills the tasks require: *analysis, comparison, evaluation, problem-solution, cause and effect, definition, description, procedural-sequential,* and *synthesis.* For example, one task template for evaluation using research reads as follows:

> After researching _____ (informational texts) on _____ (content), write a/an _____ (essay or substitute) that discusses _____ (content) and evaluates _____ (content). Be sure to support your position with evidence from your research.

Employed in a 5th grade social studies class, the task might be this:

> After researching <u>primary and secondary sources</u> on the <u>American Revolution,</u> write an <u>essay</u> that discusses <u>the American and British perspectives at the time</u> and evaluates <u>the reasons for the starting the war.</u> Be sure to support your position with evidence from your research.

When planning independent learning tasks, teachers should consider the following questions (Frey, Fisher, & Gonzalez, 2010):

1. *What digital and print-based information do students need to* ***find****?* Identify new content they will need to acquire (e.g., facts, statistics, ideas) and how they'll track down that content (e.g., with a search engine, through a WebQuest, via a personal interview).

2. *What digital and print-based information do students need to* ***use****?* Identify what students have already created or encountered in class that they will need for task completion (e.g., notes taken, annotations, course readings, video and audio recordings) and the procedures they will follow to use this material appropriately (e.g., to avoid plagiarism, to ensure proper referencing).

3. *What digital and print-based information or products do students need to **create**?* Identify the format or formats they will use to demonstrate their new learning (e.g., digital storytelling, website, presentation, written content).

4. *What digital and print-based information do students need to **share**?* Identify the ways in which students will share their information, learning, or creation with a larger audience (e.g., a review on Amazon.com, YouTube video, blog posting, or presentation).

"Independent" doesn't mean a task that's a free-for-all; the work in this phase, like all phases, must be purposeful. Asking and answering these four questions is a way that teachers can ensure students have what they need in terms of materials and directions so that they can work on their own to apply learning and don't need to keep asking what to do next. When the task is clear and the materials are readily available, teachers can be more confident that student confusion or stalling suggests they're not yet ready to work on their own and may benefit from cycling back through another phase of the framework. In addition to the planning function they serve, asking these questions supports formative assessment efforts as well as reteaching.

Independent Learning Outside School

So far we have discussed learning exclusively in terms of what happens inside the four walls of the classroom. But independent learning continues outside a teacher's company, even when it's work on a task that the teacher has designed personally. At this point, you cross your fingers and trust in the process. One kind of out-of-school independent learning is probably as old as formal schooling itself: homework. The other, blended learning, is wholly of this century. Yet both rely on cognitive, metacognitive, and self-regulatory skills we advocate teaching each day.

Homework

Few topics in education are more contentious than homework. Our students' parents tend to focus on what homework was like for them when they were students, or they discuss the effect that homework has on their home life now. Even among teachers, the subject of homework can divide faculties. Some will recount their attempts to reduce homework only to be pressured to restore it by families who equate homework with rigor. Others will justify the practice by citing the character-building attributes of completing homework or by talking about homework's academic benefits. Research suggests that homework does have a positive effect on achievement, albeit one correlated with the age of the student: the effect is smallest in the elementary school years, grows modestly in middle school, and is most closely linked to achievement in high school (Cooper, Robinson, & Patall, 2006).

There is more to homework than its effect on achievement, of course. Self-regulation is essential for all learning, and homework is a time to self-regulate (Xu & Wu, 2013). Secondary students learn that homework can contribute to their learning because they see the progress they make on summative assessments, and homework can help even primary grade students develop skills related to task completion, persistence, and memory formation.

However, children's homework does have an impact on family life, and Vatterott (2009) is among those advising teachers to keep developmental, family, and learning concerns in mind. For example, teachers might make younger students' homework assignments *time based* rather than *task based* (e.g., ask kindergarteners to complete 10 minutes of nightly homework rather than a particular worksheet). This advice certainly resonates with us. We work in a neighborhood where many students have religious and community obligations on weeknights, and one way we try to help them manage homework is to assign homework on a flexible schedule. Homework assignments are given with an expectation that they should be completed sometime during the week, but the specific night is left to the discretion of the student. Not only does this approach help students manage the expectations of home and school, but we believe it more closely parallels the demands of college and career, where task completion planning is an essential skill.

Our primary concern with homework is that it is traditionally assigned too early in the instructional cycle—before students are really ready to assume cognitive responsibility. If you follow the logic of presenting information to students and fostering those skills using a gradient of scaffolds and supports, you'll come to the same conclusion we have: *traditional homework occurs too early in the instructional cycle.* (We said it twice to emphasize the point.) It makes no sense to introduce a topic at 8:20 a.m. and then expect students to be able to do it alone, away from any support, 10 or 12 hours later. Students who are just learning a new skill—say, learning to convert fractions to decimals—are not going to be able to perform that skill very well on their own. If you release responsibility for this learning too early by making it the basis for a homework assignment, it's likely your students will reveal themselves to be one of four types:

- The *completers,* who do the homework flawlessly because a parent or older sibling was there to provide the necessary scaffolding;
- The *neglecters,* who don't do the homework for whatever reason (and you have no idea what that reason is);
- The *pleasers,* who want to make you happy so they do the homework alone, even though they don't really know how and might make a lot of errors; and
- The *cheaters,* who copy their homework from another student.

Doug freely admits to having been in the "cheater" category as a student and argues that behind every cheater is a pleaser who cares about how the teacher feels. He and a friend routinely traded homework on the long bus ride home, with Doug doing the English assignments and his friend taking charge of the mathematics ones.

Think about the consequences here. Think about the faulty data you're getting and how this affects your ability to formatively assess. You can't tell how much scaffolding the completers needed. You don't know whether any of the neglecters mastered the skills or not, because you have nothing to look at. While you can analyze the errors of the pleasers, you can't be certain the errors are really their own. What if they are actually cheaters and got help from someone who didn't really understand the material? And finally, you don't know who the cheaters are. So every morning you review last night's homework, reteaching because some students didn't get it and others didn't do it. And every morning you fall a bit further behind because you're now regularly repurposing instructional minutes for homework checking and reteaching.

To be clear, we're not homework haters. In fact, we fall into the camp that thinks homework offers valuable opportunities for learning and self-regulation. But we have found that homework works *best* when it's used to support specific aims within the instructional cycle. For example:

• *Fluency-building* homework allows students to practice skills they know well. Reading for 15 or 20 minutes per night is a great example of fluency building. Timed mathematics facts is another. This is essentially asking students to chart how many multiplication facts they can complete in one minute so they can see their fluency increase over time.

• *Spiral review* homework is designed to activate background knowledge necessary for the new skills or concepts being taught during the school day. For example, during a chemistry unit on thermal conductivity, the homework might focus on previously taught information on covalent and ionic bonds and polarity.

• *Application* homework provides learners with the chance to apply newly learned skills to a new situation. The English teachers at our school assign all students a quarterly homework assignment that requires them to attend a play, movie, or museum exhibition and write about its connection to their English content learning.

• *Extension* homework requires students to consolidate what they have learned across two or more content areas in order to deepen their knowledge. A favorite example of extension homework is the assignment given to middle school students who had learned about persuasive writing in English class and natural resources in science class to write to their city council with comments on a proposed water desalination plant.

Note that only application homework and extension homework are truly "independent learning" as defined in the gradual release of responsibility instructional framework. Fluency building and spiral review can be completed with peers, as in collaborative learning, or with adult scaffolding, as in guided instruction.

By following a purposeful approach to homework assignments, we have significantly increased the homework accuracy and completion rates. Our students often mention that the assignments are doable because they know the content and don't need to rely on others to help them. They also note that they see the connection between the homework and what they're learning in class. "It helps me [in math] when the homework is something I have to use the next day," Sha'veha told us. "There's lots of stuff to forget because I haven't used it in a while, and this is a good reminder. Keeps me fresh, you know?"

Figure 5.1 offers some reflective questions that can help teachers develop effective homework assignments.

Figure 5.1	Developing Effective Homework Assignments	
Purpose of Homework	**Characteristics**	**Reflective Questions**
Fluency building	• Multiple opportunities for practice • Focuses on one or two skills • Serves as an access point for other skills or knowledge	1. Do students fully understand how the skill is performed? 2. Is the difficulty level low enough so that they can focus on speed/rate/fluency, instead of how it is performed?
Application	• Allows a skill to be used to solve a problem, or apply a rule or principle • Uses previously learned skill for a new situation	1. What rule or principle will the students use to solve the problem? 2. Do the students possess the background knowledge and prior experiences necessary to understand the new or novel situation?
Spiral review	• Student utilizes previously learned skills or knowledge • Allows student to confirm their understanding and assess their own learning • Related conceptually to current learning	1. What previously taught skills or knowledge are important for future learning and assessment? 2. In what ways will this strengthen students' metacognitive awareness of how well they use skills and knowledge? 3. What previously taught skills or knowledge serve as a basis for current classroom instruction?
Extension	• Potential for development of new understandings • Results in a new product or innovation • Requires the use of a variety of skills or knowledge	1. Does the assignment lead to a new knowledge base or set of concepts? 2. Will the students create a new product or innovation that they have not done before? 3. What skills or knowledge will students require to complete the assignment?

Source: "Homework and the Gradual Release of Responsibility: Making 'Responsibility' Possible," by D. Fisher & N. Frey (p. 43). Copyright 2008 by the National Council of Teachers of English. Used with permission.

Blended Learning

The Common Core State Standards may articulate a progression of skills and concepts that traverse the divide between K–12 education and postsecondary applications, but students are often not prepared to tackle the independent learning required in the blended classroom and digital learning environments that they are likely to encounter in college. In fall 2010, more than 6 million college students were enrolled in at least one online course, an increase of 10 percent over the previous year and far outstripping the overall college enrollment increase rate of 2 percent (Allen & Seaman, 2011). How many college freshmen have prior experience participating in asynchronous learning environments? Do they have the skills they need to do the work expected of them?

The evolution of blended learning has its roots in the use of technology in traditional, face-to-face classroom instruction. However, true blended learning is not simply applying more technological tools to supplement brick-and-mortar learning environments; it's a blend of classroom and digital environments, with the understanding that each offers its own advantages.

Digital environments include both online learning and mobile technologies. In order for students to make the most of what blended classrooms have to offer, they need to (1) acquire the skills needed in blended learning in the face-to-face environment and then (2) parallel their learning through online coursework. Digital environments are often used in the independent learning phase of instruction, and there is an assumption that our students have a generational advantage in using the associated technology. But as we have noted throughout this chapter, effective independent learning requires attention to metacognition and self-regulation, as well as feedback from the teacher.

The skills necessary for maximizing learning opportunities in digital environments are first taught through face-to-face instruction. Enhancing classroom experiences in a purposeful and systematic way using synchronous and asynchronous digital learning helps students deepen their knowledge. In the high school where we work, 9th grade students have a full-day "field study" experience every three weeks. These events are interdisciplinary, are conducted in the community, rely on collaborative and independent learning in and out of school, and incorporate technology:

• In mathematics class, students use Geometer's Sketchpad to log coordinates (longitude and latitude) to plan field study excursions.

• In Earth Science, students use GPS location services (e.g., Google Earth) to navigate during their field study experiences.

• In Integrated Arts, students take photographs and geotag them using geospatial metadata during the field study.

• In English, students organize these images for collaborative digital storytelling (e.g., VoiceThread) after the field study.

From the time they start high school in 9th grade, all of our students' courses include a substantive asynchronous online component (e.g., discussion boards on a Haiku learning management system, Edmodo networking tools, wikis, Google Docs collaborative tools). Students continue to build their online toolkit during 10th grade, using podcasts, screencasting, video production, and screen recorders during face-to-face instruction. As they master these tools, they can use them to complete tasks outside school. Many of these tasks are collaborative and require a high degree of cooperation among students who are not in the same physical space. We use online self- and peer assessments, especially those that offer 360-degree evaluations, for these projects.

As students enter 11th grade, they are further challenged through the use of real-time (synchronous) technologies, which gives them greater access than ever before to information but also challenges them to make decisions more rapidly. To strengthen their decision-making skills, they're given additional opportunities to use real-time data in a variety of settings—using polling software to analyze statistics, for example, and participating in back-channel media technologies (interactive video commenting systems that allow for large-format public display). These back-channel media are also used in school assemblies to increase attendee participation. Our 11th grade students are tasked with managing and facilitating these parallel digital conversations.

We teach in California. In the near future, our 11th and 12th graders will be required to take at least one fully online course for credit. In 11th grade, this course will be assigned to ensure that they are meeting graduation requirements. In 12th grade, provided they meet eligibility requirements, students will propose a course enrollment based on personal interest. Eligible seniors will be encouraged to select from open courseware providers such as the Massachusetts Institute of Technology and Harvard University. They will have the option of accessing support by completing courses on campus in the computer lab or from home.

Seniors also create digital media displays of information for résumés in their English class. The Common Core standards call for students at this age to be able to make sophisticated use of digital media for the purposes of representing information. Twelfth grade students design and maintain personal websites that focus on their academic and professional experiences (four years of health internships, community college coursework, high school academics, work experiences, community service) and represent the student as a young adult preparing for the world of college and career. These websites include a blog, digital résumé, short videos of introduction, time lines, and other information appropriate for an audience of college recruiters and employers.

The Teacher's Role in Independent Learning

As students engage in independent learning, the teacher's role is to notice ongoing performance and provide feedback. Feedback is what allows students to calibrate the gap between their current state and where they want to be. It's what helps them make decisions about the allocation of attention and resources and helps them resolve problems when they are stuck. All too often, unfortunately, the feedback students receive does no such thing—primarily because it focuses on current performance to the exclusion of what could or should happen next. Keep in mind that independent learning is not synonymous with perfection; it's the journey to get to perfection. Similarly, grades are not feedback; they may be evaluative, but they do not promote further learning. Feedback occurs during independent learning, not at the end of it.

When we consider how often feedback fails to promote learning, it's instructive to consider Lee's (2009) study comparing 26 middle and high school writing instructors' expressed beliefs about feedback to the actual feedback they provided on student writing. Lee found that these teachers

- Favored focusing feedback on student strengths but actually focused their feedback primarily on weaknesses and errors;

- Expressed a belief that there is more to good writing than accuracy but focused their feedback on language form;

- Used error codes even though they confessed their students were not consistently able to decipher, understand, or apply these codes;

- Assigned and graded writing as a single attempt, even though they believed that multiple revisions are necessary to develop writing ability; and

- Continued to provide feedback as they had always done, even though they believed it had little effect.

This last point is especially troubling because it illustrates a certain resignation: teachers have given up on using feedback as a tool for improvement; for many, giving feedback is something they do more out of habit and tradition than for any defined reason. "Students cannot learn from the mistakes," said one teacher in Lee's study (2009, p. 18), yet 91 percent of the written feedback these teachers generated focused on errors.

Types of Feedback

The fact is, like pretty much anything else, feedback to students can either be done very badly or be used quite effectively. In their seminal review of the research on feedback, Hattie and Timperley (2007) describe four levels of feedback, some more effective than others:

• *Feedback about the task,* sometimes called *corrective feedback,* can be effective, but only when the student's error is due to an incorrect interpretation. When the student lacks knowledge, feedback about the task is ineffective.

• *Feedback about the processes used in the task* is more effective, as it prompts students to analyze the strategies they are using. It also mirrors the metacognitive thinking in teacher thinkalouds presented during modeling. For example, saying "This would be a good time to check the date of this historical document so you can get a better sense of what was occurring politically at the time" provides the learner with a direction to follow.

• *Feedback about self-regulation* generally draws on learners' self-efficacy—their belief in their own ability to act upon their learning. This type of feedback is also very effective, as it can build self-determination, persistence, and resilience in students. "I can see by this lab report you wrote that your hard work and studying are really paying off" is feedback that communicates the learner's control over the learning. Feedback on self-regulation need not be confined to successes, however. Consider how "You're still having trouble with explaining the differences between mitosis and meiosis, so be sure to target this area for study before the exam" directs the student to the error while building a sense of agency.

* *Feedback about the self as a person,* or general praise ("Nice job!"), does not improve learning, build agency, or change behavior. Hattie and Timperley (2007) include this kind of feedback in their article to highlight its ineffectiveness. Even when it is well meaning, feedback about the self as a person can have a negative effect. For example, "You're so smart!" reinforces a fixed mindset of ability that incorrectly leads students to believe that intelligence is innate (Dweck, 2010).

The sum takeaway is that feedback on the process a student used to complete a task promotes metacognition and feedback focused on the student's actions fosters self-regulation and a sense of autonomy. Corrective feedback about the task is effective if it is presented within the context of the next steps the student can take, and then only when it addresses a misinterpretation of a concept or skill rather than a lack of knowledge. Feedback focused on the student as a person is not effective for promoting learning.

Criteria for Feedback

Knowing the types of feedback that are most useful is an important part of the equation, but even the most effective type of feedback will be useless unless it is timely, specific, understandable, and actionable (Wiggins, 1998).

Timely. Feedback should always be paired as closely as possible to the task itself. We all have memories of receiving feedback from a teacher weeks after submitting an assignment. Any comments that might have supported the metacognitive or self-regulatory elements of learning were negated simply because too much time had passed. Feedback has to reach students when they're still in that learning space.

Specific. Vague or ambiguous feedback leaves the learner bewildered and unsure of what to do next. Give specific feedback about what is correct or what has been done well and about where improvement should occur. As an example, take a look at 3rd grade teacher Elena Anders's feedback on Corrine's diagram of the solar system:

> I can see you've got all the planets in the correct order, and all eight are here. An error I see is that the sizes are not correct. You have Venus and Mercury the same size, but Mercury is actually much smaller. I'd like for you to reread page 83 in your science book, about the sizes of the planets, and then let's look at your diagram again.

Ms. Anders's specific feedback alerts Corrine to the elements that are correct as well as those that Corrine *needs* to correct.

Understandable. Whether the feedback is understandable or not can affect its impact on learning. The meaning of feedback can be particularly elusive when the student is young, is learning a new language, or does not share a similar definition of quality as the teacher. Rubrics can be incredibly helpful in these cases, but only when the rubric is shared and discussed in advance of the independent task and only when they are not so task-specific that they become prescriptive.

A well-designed rubric defines quality across several dimensions (the columns) and describes a range of execution (the rows). It does not equate a lack of quality exclusively with the absence of an element. For example, it is common in some rubrics for the highest level of excellence to be described using a string of relative adverbs linked to frequency (always/sometimes/never). Although frequency can be a relevant element of quality, it is not the only one. For a student struggling to understand what quality execution looks like, descriptions of "poor" quality that refer to the absence of something are unlikely to be very helpful.

Actionable. Finally, feedback should result in action—and by now we hope you agree that this criterion is the most important. Feedback should be such that the student knows what to do next and has the opportunity to do it. Part of the vision statement of our high school in San Diego is that it is never too late to learn (Fisher, Frey, & Pumpian, 2012). Although we realize that time is finite and that the school year does eventually end, policy and practice dictate that assignments and competencies (assessments) be constructed to allow for revision and retakes.

At our school, building in time for post-feedback action requires teachers to think about timelines and the scheduling of units of instruction. It also requires that there be structures in place to make this additional planning work possible. We have committed to sustaining instruction until all students have met the criteria for mastery, which means teachers must think very carefully about differentiation. What should occur for students who are learning more quickly and would benefit from further extension? How do we ensure there is time and space for students who need more attention? In classrooms at our school, differentiation commonly happens during collaborative learning. While some students are receiving more teacher-directed instruction, others are extending and deepening their knowledge as they pursue even higher learning targets. Just because students have met the 6th grade social studies standards regarding ancient Mesopotamia doesn't mean the topic's exhausted. How about challenging those students to link what they have learned in class to the geopolitical climate of today?

It's not just students who benefit from good feedback. The practice of making feedback timely, specific, understandable, and actionable benefits teachers' formative instructional practices enormously. Think of the feedback you give as data for you to utilize. The challenge is to make feedback work for you as an instructor in a way that's similar to how it works for your learners.

Formative Assessment During the Independent Learning Phase

Each of the phases of instruction we have looked at so far incorporates some means of checking for understanding. To recap:

- During *focused instruction,* the teacher indicates where students are going in their learning by establishing the purpose, modeling and thinking aloud as an expert, and noticing students' initial understandings.
- During *guided instruction,* the teacher utilizes what she has noticed to scaffold student understanding through questions, prompts, and cues.
- During *collaborative learning,* the teacher gauges how well students appear to be consolidating and extending their learning and provides course corrections as needed.

Now, during *independent learning,* the teacher's role is to check in with students as they move forward on their own, noticing this progress and ensuring students receive that serves to refine and deepen understanding.

That's not to say that all independent learning tasks are formative; many are summative and are appropriately used for grading and evaluation. Appropriate summative assessments occur after numerous rounds of formative assessment, error analysis, and reteaching based on the patterns identified. Although both formative and summative assessment have a place in schooling, teachers intent on moving students toward better learning use student performance data to guide their instruction. We can create a feed-forward system so that student performance data can be used informatively (Fisher & Frey, 2012d).

Know the Difference Between Mistakes and Errors

When a student inaccurately interprets something due to inattention to the task (e.g., forgets an important step), that student is making a mistake, not an error. You know you're dealing with a mistake when you give corrective feedback and immediately see the proverbial light bulb go on. As noted, corrective feedback is useful when students have knowledge. Once corrected, they realize what they need to do next, and the teacher gives them the time and space to do it. Independent learning continues as planned.

An error, on the other hand, is a signal that an adjustment is needed. Errors are what you're dealing with when you give students corrective feedback about a task or about the processes they need to employ and you get a blank stare in return. They simply don't know what you're talking about. Their lack of knowledge or their misconceptions mean that your corrective feedback isn't enough to get learning on track. These students need a return to focused instruction or additional guided instruction, and you need to adjust your plans accordingly.

Track Errors and Find Error Patterns

Most of us have had the experience of stopping the class during a task because we have detected a pattern in the questions coming from students. When the fourth child in as many minutes asks the same question about the directions, it's a neon sign that the whole class would benefit from clarification.

Unfortunately, it's rare for a teacher to get so clear a signal. Elementary teachers spend six or seven hours a day in the company of their students, and it can be very difficult to recall who needed more help with multiplying fractions when they are also responsible for teaching language arts, science, and the visual and performing arts. Secondary teachers have the opposite problem. Although the scope of their content teaching is more limited, they are seeing 150 or more students a day. Who can keep track?

One solution is to use a simple error analysis sheet (see Figure 5.2) to record all the information coming in. After identifying the major skills or concepts that have been taught, teachers can jot down the initials of the students who are making errors and require further instruction in the identified areas.

Figure 5.2	Error Analysis Sheet				
Date: _10/12_ Topic: _"What Sustains Us?" draft essay; focus on mechanics_					
Error	**Period 1**	**Period 2**	**Period 3**	**Period 4**	**Period 5**
Mid-sentence capitalization	JC			AA	
Colons and semicolons	JC, JT, AG, DL, TV	EC, MV, WK		AA, SK, MG, EM, BA, TS	HH, DP, MR, CH
Ending punctuation	JC, AG, SL	WK, MW		AA, BA	MR
Subject–verb	JC, JT, DL, MM, SL, ST, ND	RT, VE, VD, CC		AA, MG, SC, PM, LG	DP, DE
Tense consistency	DS	SJ, JM		AA, TR, PC	DE
Spelling	JC, MM	WK, RT, AG, SJ		AA, MG, BA, GL, PT, DO, DE, LR	SR, DC, MF

Distinguish Between Targeted and Global Errors (and Teach Accordingly)

Using an error analysis sheet helps us figure out what kinds of instructional adjustments need to be made. In the case of the draft essay in Figure 5.2, we are able to see precisely who needs to be in small-group focused or guided instruction. In other cases, we notice that one of the cells on the form is filling up with initials, which signals that some whole-group instruction addressing these specific skills or concepts would be beneficial. This kind of global error might show up within a single class period of students or at times involves students in several periods. Either way, it means that teachers need to examine the overall instructional design to figure out why the original plan didn't work—or didn't work in particular classes.

Tracking errors is important because it prevents us from reteaching the entire class because we can't recall who needed help. When a large number of students across periods don't make progress, error analysis prevents us from sticking with a flawed instructional plan and may suggest a need to redesign the overall unit of study.

Conclusion

As we have noted, independent learning is *not* "do-it-yourself school." Students should be engaged in tasks that require them to apply what they have learned and that allow them to ask new questions about the world around them. Independent learning should build students' metacognitive skills while allowing the teacher to determine areas of additional instructional need. In other words, although independent learning is a critical aspect of the gradual release of responsibility instructional framework, it's one that has been neglected.

As Cain (2012) notes, "If solitude is an important key to creativity—then we might all want to develop a taste for it. We'd want to teach our kids to work independently" (p. 75). Given the demands on students, whether because of the Common Core State Standards or the requirements of blended learning, they must learn to rally their experience, prioritize their tasks, and get to work. When they do so, we will have successfully released responsibility (at least for some amount of content) to our students. Only then will they develop the expertise necessary to succeed in college, their career, and life.

Implementing the Gradual Release of Responsibility Instructional Framework

Perhaps the gradual release of responsibility instructional framework we have described is similar to the instructional design process you already use in your classroom; perhaps it is quite different. In this final chapter, we will focus on issues of implementation, particularly planning with and introducing this framework to your students. We will also address what peers and administrators should look for in a classroom structured in this way. And, finally, we will share some important questions to ask yourself as you implement a gradual release of responsibility model in your own classroom.

Although we have presented this framework in a sequential manner, implementation is not a strictly linear process. It is not necessary to march directly from focused instruction to guided instruction and then to collaborative learning, holding independent learning until the very end of the unit. A given lesson may start with any phase of the instructional framework, as when a lesson begins with an inquiry-based collaborative learning task. Likewise, certain instructional moves may occur multiple times within the same lesson, as when a teacher establishes several different purposes to reflect a shift in instructional focus from one concept or skill to another. Remember, learning is recursive and iterative, and every lesson occurs within a larger instructional context. Students will continually need to recall, apply, and further existing skills and knowledge as part of the process of acquiring new skills and knowledge.

Gradual Release of Responsibility Is Consistent with Other Research-Based Approaches

Our instructional practices have been profoundly influenced by Tomlinson and Imbeau's (2010) differentiation of instruction, Wiggins and McTighe's (2005) Understanding by Design (UbD®) process, and Popham's (2008) take on formative and transformative assessment. We use these processes in developing units of study for our students, and aspects of each are integrated into the gradual release of responsibility instructional framework.

Differentiated Instruction and Gradual Release

Carol Tomlinson's framework for differentiation describes a process for considering the learning styles, abilities, and interests of learners in order to create educational experiences that balance challenge with success. As we discussed in Chapter 3, these experiences can be differentiated in one or more aspects of the curriculum: content, process, and product. As Tomlinson and others (e.g., Benjamin, 2002) have noted, some educators see the implementation of differentiated instruction as problematic because their reliance on whole-group instruction doesn't allow time for students to work at different rates, on a variety of topics, or with a range of materials.

The gradual release of responsibility model has been our solution to the logistics of differentiation. Focused instruction provides time to introduce new concepts for all students and to ensure they are all exposed to grade-level thinking. It is in the guided instruction, collaborative learning, and independent learning phases of the framework that differentiation takes place. We can group students homogeneously for guided instruction that is customized to their learning needs, then regroup them heterogeneously for peer learning. At times, collaborative learning also becomes homogeneous, as when students are grouped by interest or task preference. Learners also work independently to demonstrate their mastery of a concept or skill. Learning contracts, curriculum compacting, and tiered assignments and tests all factor into the educational experiences of our students.

Understanding by Design and Gradual Release

The UbD process developed by Grant Wiggins and Jay McTighe (2005) features three major components:

- Identifying desired results,
- Determining acceptable evidence, and
- Planning learning experiences and instruction.

Determining the enduring understandings of learning is invaluable in developing the units of study. In particular, the essential questions posed throughout a unit keep us and our students centered on the purpose of the learning. The process's tools also help us to plan the assessments we will use.

The gradual release of responsibility instructional framework aligns well with the third step in the UbD process: planning learning experiences and instruction. The recursive aspects of the framework provide teachers with an instructional design process that allows them to plan learning experiences that transfer the cognitive load to students over time while also being able to differentiate those experiences. Of course, instructional design is meaningless without units of study that possess the rigor of enduring understandings and a clear structure of formative and summative assessments to check for understanding (Fisher & Frey, 2007a).

Formative Assessment and Gradual Release

Assessments are used in school for many reasons:

- To assist student learning;
- To identify students' strengths and weaknesses;
- To assess the effectiveness of a particular instructional strategy;
- To assess and improve the effectiveness of curriculum programs;
- To assess and improve teaching effectiveness;
- To provide data that assist in decision making; and
- To communicate with and involve parents. (Kellough & Kellough, 1999, pp. 418–419)

These purposes can be organized into three main types of assessment: *diagnostic, formative,* and *summative.* In general, diagnostic assessments are used to identify student weakness or for students to qualify for special programs. Teachers use formative assessment to plan subsequent instruction. As Popham (2008) reminds us, assessments can be used to inform, and transform, our instruction. Summative assessments are evaluative and typically high-stakes; they are designed to summarize what a student has learned.

According to the National Council of Teachers of Mathematics' *Principles and Standards for School Mathematics* (2000):

> Assessment should be more than merely a test at the end of instruction to see how students perform under special conditions; rather, it should be an integral part of instruction that

informs and guides teachers as they make instructional decisions. Assessment should not merely be done *to* students; rather, it should also be done *for* students, to guide and enhance their learning. (The Assessment Principle, ¶1)

When teachers are gradually releasing responsibility to students, formative assessment is especially critical. Guided instruction is dependent on insight into students' learning status; it's how teachers form groups and how they decide what to teach to these groups. We also know that the systematic use of formative assessment data improves student achievement. Black and Wiliam's (1998) analysis of findings from 250 journal articles and book chapters concluded that the regular use of formative assessment raises academic achievement. Classrooms that use formative assessment data to flexibly group students use a *situational* process, meaning that students are taught first and then grouped for reteaching or extension, based on the most current information. Mason and Good (1993) compared the effects of both approaches on mathematics learning with 1,700 intermediate students and found that learners in the situational approach outperformed those in classrooms that used a structural approach.

Planning with the Gradual Release of Responsibility Instructional Framework

After identifying units of study, teachers plan a series of lessons. A number of different tools can support the thoughtful engagement required of our framework's structured teaching. Our lesson plan template (see Figure 6.1), for example, contains guiding questions to assist in planning. Figure 6.2 shows a lesson plan that Brandon Carmichael developed for his middle school social studies students, using our template. Let's take a look at both the template and what Mr. Carmichael has done with it.

Figure 6.1 Lesson Plan Template

Topic/Theme/Unit:

Standards Addressed:

Essential Questions:

Purpose(s)—Content, Language, and Social:

Materials/Resources:

FOCUSED INSTRUCTION

"I DO IT"

How will you...

☐ Make lesson purposes (content-language-social) clear to your students?

☐ Connect to prior learning?

☐ Ensure relevance and interest in the content?

☐ Model and demonstrate?

☐ Notice what students are learning and still need to learn?

☐ Provide multiple explanations for new concepts?

☐ Allow for student interaction?

GUIDED INSTRUCTION	"WE DO IT"
How will you . . . ☐ Know that each student thought through and formulated a response to questions? ☐ Prompt and cue as needed? ☐ Allow students a variety of methods and modalities in which to respond? ☐ Assist students in processing information?	

COLLABORATIVE LEARNING	"YOU DO IT TOGETHER"
How will you . . . ☐ Determine the complexity of the task? ☐ Provide students with hands-on experiences and practice? ☐ Determine grouping (pairs, groups) for this activity? ☐ Ensure that students have sufficient language support to be successful in collaborative tasks? ☐ Hold students accountable for their learning?	

(continued)

Figure 6.1   Lesson Plan Template (*continued*)

INDEPENDENT LEARNING	"YOU DO IT ALONE"
How will you	
❑ Intervene with students who are not ready to move on?	
❑ Assess at the close of the lesson to determine who has mastered content and who needs further assistance?	
❑ Extend the lesson for those who are ready to move on?	
❑ Support students in connecting concepts to future lessons and in exploring real-life applications?	
❑ Provide opportunities for students to self-assess?	
❑ Offer opportunities for students to extend their learning?	
❑ Endorse independent learning or more in-depth study of content by students?	

ASSESSMENT	
Formative:	Summative:

Figure 6.2   Sample Lesson Plan

Topic/Theme/Unit:
Immigration and the Immigrant Experience

Purpose(s)—Content, Language, and Social:
Content Goal: Understand that immigration in America is long standing and complicated.
Language Goals: Interpret two types of documents: (1) a written report (secondary source); (2) images (photographs); practice writing a conversation; complete "I Am" poem.
Social Goals: Equitable participation and openness to other points of view.

Materials/Resources:
Textbook
Copies/digital access to the following:
- "The Peopling of America, 1830–1930" timeline and commentary downloaded from www.ellisis land.org
- The written document analysis and photo analysis worksheets from www.archives.gov
- Photographs of Ellis Island and Angel Island immigrants
- "Brief on Appeal" and "Angel Island Poem #32"
- "Mexican Workers await legal employment in the United States, Mexicali (Mexico)" and "Library of Congress (LOC) Mexican Immigration"
- "Children at work" images from http://www.archives.gov/education/lessons/hine-photos/#documents

Standards Addressed:

California History—Social Science Content Standards
Chronological & Spatial Thinking 1: Students explain how major events are related to one another over time.
8.12: Students analyze the transformation of the American Economy and the changing social and political conditions in the United States in response to the Industrial Revolution.

Common Core ELA/Literacy Standards
Reading Informational Text: Key Ideas and Details
RI.8.1: Cite the textual evidence that mostly strongly supports an analysis of what the text says explicitly as well as inferences drawn from the text.
Reading Informational Text: Craft and Structure
RI.8.4: Determine the meaning of words and phrases as they are used in a text, including figurative, connotative, and technical meanings; analyze the impact of specific word choices on meaning and tone, including analogies or allusions to other texts.
RI.8.5: Analyze in detail the structure of a specific paragraph in a text, including the role of particular sentences in developing and refining a key concept.
Speaking and Listening: Comprehension and Collaboration
SL.8.1: Engage effectively in a range of collaborative discussions (one-on-one, in groups, and teacher-led) with diverse partners on grade 8 topics, texts, and issues, building on others' ideals and expressing their own clearly.
SI.8.2: Analyze the purpose of information presented in diverse media and formats (e.g. visually, quantitatively, orally) and evaluate the motives (e.g., social, commercial, political) behind its presentation.

(continued)

Figure 6.2   Sample Lesson Plan (*continued*)

Essential Questions:
How have immigrants contributed to America's economy?

How are immigrants' experiences similar?

	"I DO IT"
How will you... ☑ Make lesson purposes (content-language-social) clear to your students? ☑ Connect to prior learning? ☑ Ensure relevance and interest in the content? ☑ Model and demonstrate? ☑ Notice what students are learning and still need to learn? ☑ Provide multiple explanations for new concepts? ☑ Allow for student interaction?	**FOCUSED INSTRUCTION** Teacher shares the purpose with students and checks their understanding by asking for random students to retell the purpose. Teacher notes the relevance of this learning, given the continued debates about immigration. Teacher also notes the learning thus far related to immigration policies and history. Teacher reads aloud an overview of U.S. immigration and immigration patterns from the Ellis Island web page ("The Peopling of America, 1830–1930"). All students receive a copy to follow along with. Read the selection twice, once straight through to get the overall ideas and a second time with an emphasis on making understanding and questions transparent. For the second read-aloud, teacher models metacognition strategies, thinking aloud about (1) what documents would help build a better understanding of the immigrant experience; and (2) if the experience the same for immigrants entering the United States through Ellis Island, through the West Coast, and from the southern borders of California, Arizona, and Texas. Teacher displays the resources each of the groups will be receiving to provide a bigger picture of the work for the day, and then assigns the groups their particular document. Teacher makes connection between the new tool (a photo analysis worksheet from the National Archives (with a previously used analysis tool) the written document analysis worksheet from same). Students talk with one another about the photo analysis.

GUIDED INSTRUCTION	"WE DO IT"

How will you . . .

☑ Know that each student thought through and formulated a response to questions?

☑ Prompt and cue as needed?

☑ Allow students a variety of methods and modalities in which to respond?

☑ Assist students in processing information?

Whole-Group Guided Instruction

Teacher reviews purpose and use of the photo analysis worksheet.

Teacher discusses and defines two main aspects of interpretation: (1) observation and (2) speculation/interpretation.

Small-Group Guided Instruction

The group evaluates two pictures, one of immigrants arriving at Ellis Island and another of immigrants landing at Angel Island.

1. Students complete a photo analysis worksheet for each picture.
2. Students discuss similarities and differences between the two pictures.
3. Students write a paragraph on the back of the photo analysis worksheet reflecting on this prompt: "Based upon these two pictures, the people are prepared to work." Each member will be responsible for reporting on the group's work.

Small-Group Guided Instruction

The group evaluates two documents: "Brief on Appeal" and "Angel Island Poem #32."

1. Students complete a document analysis worksheet for each document.
2. Students highlight and discuss any words they find in the documents they believe are "loaded" or point to evidence of the author having a slanted or predisposed social, commercial, or political view of the situation described.
3. Students chart (on an overhead transparency) five specific words they discussed and prepare to present these ideas to a class, via a spokesperson.

Small-Group Guided Instruction

"As needed" error analysis based on difficulty reading textbook-like secondary sources.

1. Students examine the documents "Mexican Workers Await Legal Employment in the United States, Mexicali (Mexico)" and "Library of Congress (LOC) Mexican Immigration."
2. Students highlight words they don't understand and main ideas.
3. Students number the ideas in order; how does the author use one sentence or idea as a basis for the next point?
4. With a partner, students complete a silent (written) conversation.

Small-Group Guided Instruction

"As needed" misconception analysis based on previous use of the document analysis worksheet.

1. Students review "Children at Work" (from the textbook), an illustration from the textbook, and a "children at work" image from the National Archives and Records Administration.
2. Teacher assists students in completing the document analysis worksheets for the textbook example (text and images).
3. Students complete a photograph analysis worksheet analyzing the image from the National Archives.
4. Students complete an "I Am" poem.

(continued)

Figure 6.2 Sample Lesson Plan (*continued*)

How will you . . .	COLLABORATIVE LEARNING	"YOU DO IT TOGETHER"
☑ Determine the complexity of the task?	**Collaborative Task 1:** One member from each small group explains one point from one of the documents or photographs examined. Together, the collaborative group completes the sentence: "Immigrants enter America with the expectation. . . . "	
☑ Provide students with hands-on experiences and practice?	**Collaborative Task 2:** One member from each small group explains one point from one of the documents or photographs examined. Students create a thesis statement that presents the immigrants' point of view and justifies immigrating; what were the "pull factors" for immigrants?	
☑ Determine grouping (pairs, groups) for this activity?	**Collaborative Task 3:** One member from each small group explains one point from one of the documents or photographs examined. Students agree on one major point to complete the sentence: "One reason people come to America is. . . . "	
☑ Ensure that students have sufficient language support to be successful in collaborative tasks?	**Collaborative Task 4:** One member from each small group explains one point from one of the documents or photographs examined. Students create a thesis statement that reflects a valid point of view from an immigrant official denying entry on the West Coast.	
☑ Hold students accountable for their learning?		

INDEPENDENT LEARNING	"YOU DO IT ALONE"
How will you . . . . ☑ Intervene with students who are not ready to move on? ☑ Assess at the close of the lesson to determine who has mastered content and who needs further assistance? ☑ Extend the lesson for those who are ready to move on? ☑ Support students in connecting concepts to future lessons and in exploring real-life applications? ☑ Provide opportunities for students to self-assess? ☑ Offer opportunities for students to extend their learning? ☑ Endorse independent learning or more in-depth study of content by students?	**Independent Task 1:** Students complete "silent conversation" ticket out the door: "I Am" poem. **Independent Task 2:** Students read the textbook selection on immigration in the United States and prepare Cornell notes. **Independent Task 3:** Students ready to move on watch a History Channel video and then prepare and deliver a peer lesson based on the video content. Students who are not ready to move on learning will receive additional guided instruction.

ASSESSMENT	
Formative: Exit tickets (2) Short essay explaining the benefits and challenges of immigration	**Summative:** Essay identifying the benefits of immigration in the late 19th century Quiz on immigration and the Industrial Revolution

Source: Developed by the Santa Clara County Office of Education, Santa Clara, California. Adapted with permission.

Topic/theme and standards. The unit of study is on immigration and the immigrant experiences, which is part of the California 8th grade standards' focus on the American economy and the Industrial Revolution. This unit also integrates several 8th grade Common Core State Standards in ELA/literacy, specifically standards RI.8.1, RI.8.4, RI.8.5, SL.8.1, and SL.8.2.

Essential question. An essential question reminds students of the overarching purpose of learning concepts. In this case, students are asked to consider the ways in which immigrants have contributed to America's economy and how immigrants' experiences are similar.

Purposes. Mr. Carmichael has identified the learning that his students need as they progress toward meeting the standard.

Focused instruction. Mr. Carmichael planned three different episodes of focused instruction. He will read aloud to his students, modeling his thinking about a text. He will model his thinking about finding additional information and then model the use of a document analysis tool produced by the National Archives.

Guided instruction. Mr. Carmichael has planned several guided instruction lessons because he doesn't do the majority of his teaching to the whole group. He has found that time spent with smaller groups of students yields great rewards because he can be much more precise. His first guided lesson is a whole-group one because he wants to be sure all students understand the tool they will be using in their own analysis. In the smaller groups, he guides students' thinking, scaffolding it through prompts and cues about the documents they are investigating.

Collaborative learning. Collaborative learning will be going on at the same time as guided instruction, so Mr. Carmichael has designed a series of activities that will extend over a few days. He knows that initial collaborative learning must be easy enough for students to complete together, so he has them work in teams on a more familiar task. Over the course of the lesson, students will collaborate on increasingly complex tasks that allow them to consolidate their understanding of the content.

Independent learning. Repetition and reinforcement are key to long-term retention of concepts and skills, so Mr. Carmichael plans to check in on students' application through three independent learning tasks: an exit slip after the first day of instruction on what they learned, an "I Am" poem, and note taking from their textbook. This gives him further insight into who understands the concepts and who still needs instruction.

Formative and summative assessment. Mr. Carmichael has designed an instructional plan that incorporates exit slips, products from the guided instruction lessons, homework, and a short essay. This provides him with the variety and authenticity he seeks in good formative assessment, and the different tasks communicate strongly to his students that learning history is more than memorizing facts and dates. His summative assessments include an end-of-chapter test from the teacher's guide accompanying the textbook series and an essay addressing the essential question.

What School Leaders Should Look for in a Gradual Release of Responsibility Classroom

As schools and districts implement the gradual release model in their classrooms, it is important to monitor indicators of success. As with UbD, identifying end results and determining acceptable evidence are essential to achieving desired outcomes (Wiggins & McTighe, 2005). Figure 6.3 provides a rubric administrators and instructional coaches can use to support teachers who are implementing a gradual release of responsibility framework.

Figure 6.3   Gradual Release of Responsibility Quality Indicators

		Phase 1: Focused Instruction		
Quality Indicator	Proficient – 4	Skillful – 3	Approaching – 2	Minimal – 1
Lesson contains content, language, and social purposes and is based on formative assessment.	• Lesson is explicitly presented through content, language, and social purposes, which are based on content standards and language demands of the task as well as students' assessed needs.	• Purposes are stated and address students' needs identified via formative assessments but are not well connected to content standards or language demands of the task.	• Only one purpose is stated (i.e., content, language, or social purpose is missing), or purpose is not relevant for students. Some type of assessment has been used to design instruction.	• No content or language purpose is stated or implied. There is no evidence of formative assessment to plan instruction.
Students can explain purposes in their own words: *what* they are learning, *how* they show their learning, and *why* they need to learn this lesson.	• Randomly selected students can explain or demonstrate how the stated purposes relate to their own learning.	• Students can accurately restate the purposes of the lesson but lack a clear understanding of why they are being taught the content.	• Students can restate portions of the purposes of the lesson but lack an understanding of why they are being taught the content.	• Students are unable to correctly state the purpose of the lesson.
Teacher provides an authentic model or demonstration while noticing student responses.	• Modeling includes naming task or strategy, explaining when used, using analogies to link to new learning. • Teacher demonstrates task or strategy, alerts of errors to avoid, shows how applied to check for accuracy. • Modeling consistently contains "I" statements and metacognitive examples. • The teacher notices how students respond and addresses student responses.	• Modeling contains all the indicators (naming, explaining, analogies, demonstration, errors to avoid, and checking), but the teacher only uses some "I" statements. • Metacognition is limited. • The teacher notices how students respond but does not address student responses.	• Modeling contains some indicators (naming, explaining), but the teacher directs students through the use of "you" statements and does not use metacognitive statements to further student understanding. • The teacher does not notice how students respond.	• Modeling contains few indicators. Teacher uses "you" or "we" statements that focus on processes, not thinking. • Student responses are ignored.

Quality Indicator	Proficient – 4	Skillful – 3	Approaching – 2	Minimal – 1
Phase 2: Guided Instruction				
Teacher scaffolds support for students using questions, prompts, and cues.	• Teacher poses questions, asks for clarification; if response is incorrect, directs student to previous learning via prompt. If response still incorrect, provides cues before moving to reinstruction.	• Teacher poses question, asks for clarification; if response is incorrect, directs student to previous learning via prompt.	• Teacher poses question and asks for clarification when response is correct (e.g., *How did you figure that out? How do you know? How did you figure that out?*), but moves to direct explanation when response is incorrect.	• Teacher poses question, and when student(s) respond incorrectly supplies the answer or moves on to next student.
Teacher differentiates instruction and practice based on formative assessment.	• Group formation is flexible and based on formative assessment from daily lessons. • Students are able to apply information based on the support provided by instruction. • Tasks differ based on students' needs and/or students' selection.	• Group formation is flexible based on formative assessments from weekly lessons. • Students apply information based on initial instruction and teacher support.	• Group formation is based on recent formative assessments but is fixed. • Tasks are similar to those presented in lesson.	• Group formation is static and based on outdated information. • Tasks are identical for each group, with no visible differentiation.
Phase 3: Collaborative Learning				
Quality Indicator	Proficient – 4	Skillful – 3	Approaching – 2	Minimal – 1
The tasks assigned accurately reflect the established purposes.	• All tasks students complete reflect the established purposes.	• Most tasks students complete reflect the established purposes.	• Some tasks students complete reflect the established purposes.	• Tasks students complete are not consistent with the stated purpose.
Students use strategies and skills that were previously modeled.	• After receiving adequate time in scaffolded instructional support, all students can complete tasks using the strategy or skill that was modeled.	• After receiving limited time in scaffolded instructional support students complete tasks using the strategy or skill that was modeled.	• Students move directly to independent learning, with little in the way of instructional support.	• There is a mismatch between what was modeled and what students are asked to do.

(continued)

Figure 6.3 Gradual Release of Responsibility Quality Indicators (*continued*)

		Phase 3: Collaborative Learning (*continued*)		
Quality Indicator	**Proficient – 4**	**Skillful – 3**	**Approaching – 2**	**Minimal – 1**
The task is appropriately complex. It is a novel application of a grade-level appropriate concept and is designed so that the outcome is not guaranteed (a chance for productive failure exists).	• Task reflects purpose(s) and allows students an opportunity to use a variety of resources to creatively apply and extend their knowledge. • Students have an opportunity to experiment with concepts. • The accountability matches the task type.	• Tasks provide opportunities for students to apply their knowledge, although the outcome is somewhat assured. • The accountability matches the task type.	• The task is somewhat reflective of the purpose of the lesson, but there is little opportunity for student experimentation or innovation. • The accountability matches the task type.	• Task is an exact replication of what was modeled with no opportunity for student experimentation with concepts. • Accountability is nonexistent or inappropriate for the task.
Small groups of 2–5 students are purposefully constructed to maximize individual strengths without magnifying areas of need.	• Groups are flexible and change based on students' proficiency, academic needs, or content area, and interest.	• Purposeful heterogeneous grouping occurs. • Groups are primarily based on students' proficiency.	• Some heterogeneous grouping occurs, but homogeneous grouping practices dominate. • Decisions based on assessments are not apparent.	• Grouping practices are solely homogeneous and are done primarily for scheduling convenience.
Students use accountable talk to persuade, provide evidence, ask questions of one another, and disagree without being disagreeable.	• Students reach a better understanding or consensus based on evidence and opinions provided by others. • Students hold each member of the group accountable by using questioning strategies and evidence to persuade or disagree. • The conversation is respectful and courteous.	• Students ask for and offer evidence to support claims. However, members continue to maintain initial beliefs or positions about a topic without considering the arguments of others. • The conversation is generally respectful but some members may not participate.	• There is a process in place for accountable talk. However, student dialogue is limited and there are minimal efforts to support statements, opinions, or claims. • The conversation is generally respectful, but is often dominated by one member of the group.	• No clear process is in place to facilitate accountable talk. • Lack of structure is evidenced by students who are off task, in conflict, or are unable to complete tasks.

Phase 4: Independent Learning

Quality Indicator	Proficient – 4	Skillful – 3	Approaching – 2	Minimal – 1
Tasks are meaningful, relevant, and an extension of the purposes for learning.	• Learning tasks provide opportunities to apply learning in unique or different situations that deepen students' learning. • The tasks are relevant and generate new questions for the learner.	• Learning tasks provide students with opportunities to apply what they have learned.	• Learning tasks mirror previous instruction rather than serve as an opportunity to apply what has been learned.	• Learning tasks are disconnected to instruction.
Teacher provides explicit feedback in order to deepen or solidify students' understanding.	• Feedback is timely, actionable, understandable, and specific. • Students are able to use feedback to improve and refine their learning. • Feedback is carefully crafted to focus on the processes used and to develop self-regulation and metacognition.	• Feedback is timely, understandable, and specific. • The feedback is carefully crafted to focus on the processes used and to develop self-regulation and metacognition. • Feedback occurs at the end of independent learning and cannot be used to improve and refine learning.	• Feedback is timely and understandable, but more general. • The feedback is primarily focused on the task, rather than processes, self-regulation, and metacognition. • Feedback occurs at the end of independent learning and cannot be used to improve and refine learning.	• Feedback is focused exclusively on correction. It may be delayed, misunderstood, and/or vague. • Feedback occurs too late to be useful in promoting student learning.
Students assumed increased responsibility for learning.	• Students self-evaluate their learning and develop next steps to increase their understanding of the content.	• Students routinely self-evaluate their learning as a reflective process rather than a proactive one.	• Students discuss their learning with peers or teacher but do not routinely self-evaluate.	• Teacher provides feedback, but students do not have time to evaluate their learning.

Questions a Teacher Should Ask

Determining where to begin in implementing a gradual release of responsibility can be daunting. We have developed these guiding questions as a way to support your efforts to integrate the framework into your existing instructional design.

Have I modeled things I expect students to do collaboratively and independently?

Many teachers assume that effective collaborative and independent learning will take care of itself, but we have discovered that explicit direction in how to work collaboratively and independently is a linchpin in a successful gradual release of responsibility classroom.

For this reason, during the first 20 days of the school year or semester, we devote some time each class period to building our students' capacity to work collaboratively and independently. We provide focused instruction on the tasks they will need to do, for example, using the classroom computers, applying a mnemonic for writing in-class essays, participating in collaborative groups, and completing independent reading assignments. After we introduce each activity, we divide the students into groups so they can practice it. For example, after we have taught two collaborative learning activities, we split the class in half and ask each group to complete a task and then switch. We spend our time circulating and assisting, monitoring behavior, and redirecting students who are off task. As we introduce new collaborative and independent tasks, we further subdivide the class. Once we have taught the major tasks, including routines and procedures, we then introduce guided instruction into the mix. Only when students have been properly prepared for collaborative and independent learning can you count on having the (relatively) uninterrupted time you'll need for small group-guided instruction.

Do I have the materials I need to engage my students?

This question relates to differentiated instruction, as you'll discover that your students need a range of materials in order to learn the content. The textbook is a great resource, but it is not the only item students should have. Bookmark websites on your classroom computers, and talk to your school librarian about the hidden treasures that are tucked away somewhere. We have worked at schools where grade levels assemble "resource kits" of specialized materials, which are stored in labeled boxes and available for checkout. These resource kits are great because they encourage all of us to dig out materials we use only once a year. You may find that you need multiple copies of some supplies, such as file folder games for young children or storage bags of math manipulatives. Elementary schools are fortunate in being able to draw on the support of family volunteers to complete this kind of project. If you are working at a middle or high school, consider promoting the creation of resource kits as a community service project for an honor society, a school club, or a young adult who is fulfilling requirements for a scholarship, diploma, or degree.

Where can I find more time for guided instruction?

You can't create more time, but you can use the time you have more effectively. A great tip is to look for occasions when what you're doing is more managerial than instructional—when you are showing a video in class, for example, or supervising independent work, watching students as they read an assignment, or walking up and down the aisles of the classroom hushing students as you go. If you recast whole-class activities that don't require your active participation to be collaborative tasks, you'll be free to spend more of your time providing guided instruction to small groups.

What can I do to ensure that independent learning tasks really are meaningful?

Like us, you probably vowed in your teacher preparation program that you would never be one of "those" teachers who gives students lots of busywork as a way to maintain order (meaning silence) in the classroom. We hope we have made a case that independent learning tasks are a critical component of a gradual release of responsibility model, but we also feel teachers really do need to examine the quality of what is traditionally used for independent work. Problem sets and questions at the end of the chapter are rarely engaging enough to keep most learners motivated. These practice-level tasks can be made more interesting by shifting them to the collaborative learning phase, giving students an opportunity to use the social and academic language they need in order to support their own learning.

Wilson and Cutting (2001) remind us that students advance their learning through

• *Finding out:* Tasks associated with Bloom's knowledge and comprehension levels;
• *Sorting out:* Tasks associated with the application and analysis levels; and
• *Speaking out:* Tasks associated with the synthesis and evaluation levels.

Although all of these levels of understanding are important, we view synthesis and evaluation as the most essential to lasting understanding. If students' independent learning tasks are clumping up at the "finding out" and "sorting out" categories to the exclusion of "speaking out" opportunities, this is a signal that you should shift those tasks to other phases of the framework: to focus lessons, guided instruction, or collaborative learning.

What classroom routines and procedures will help me teach this way?

Routines and procedures are essential in any classroom, regardless of the age of the students or the teacher's instructional approach. There should be clear routines for retrieving and putting away supplies, for example, and for turning in completed work and asking for help. In a gradual release of responsibility classroom, particularly useful routines and procedures include

- Following schedules for collaborative learning and guided instruction groups;
- Transitioning between whole-group and small-group learning;
- Maintaining an acceptable noise level; and
- Wrapping up at the end of class, including putting materials away, moving furniture, and writing down homework assignments.

Conclusion

The gradual release of responsibility instructional framework is not something that can be implemented overnight, but it can be done successfully over time. This approach complements other research-based strategies, especially differentiated instruction, the backward planning of UbD, and formative assessment. Consider the necessary routines and procedures that students will need to know, and then dedicate some time each day to providing instruction on how to work collaboratively and independently. This will make the introduction of guided instruction much smoother because students will know what is expected from them, even when you aren't standing in front of them to tell them explicitly.

As you prepare to close this book (and, we hope, share it with a friend), reconsider how *you* learn. Think about the things you're good at and about how you got good. Can you see the gradual release of responsibility instructional framework in your own learning? Can you see this approach resulting in better outcomes for students? The responsibility is now yours . . . enjoy!

References

Aldrich, C. (2005). *Learning by doing: A comprehensive guide to simulations, computer games, and pedagogy in e-learning and other educational experiences.* San Francisco: Jossey-Bass.

Allen, I. E., & Seaman, J. (2011). *Going the distance: Online education in the United States, 2011.* Babson Park, MA: Babson Survey Research Group and Quahog Research Group. Retrieved from http://www.onlinelearningsurvey.com/reports/goingthedistance.pdf

Anderson, N. J. (2002, April). *The role of metacognition in second language teaching and learning* (ERIC Digest EDO-FL-01-10). Retrieved from http://www.cal.org/resources/digest/0110anderson.html

Angelo, T. A. (1991). Ten easy pieces: Assessing higher learning in four dimensions. *Classroom Research: Early Lessons from Success, 46,* 17–31.

ASCD Whole Child Initiative. (n.d.). *Whole child tenet #3: Engaged.* Retrieved from http://www.wholechildeducation.org/assets/content/mx-resources/wholechildindicators-engaged.pdf

Atkin, B. (2000). *Voices from the fields: Children of migrant farmworkers tell their stories.* New York: Little, Brown.

Bandura, A. (1965). Influence of models' reinforcement contingencies on the acquisition of imitative responses. *Journal of Personality and Social Psychology, 1,* 589–595. Available: http://dx.doi.org/10.1037/h0022070

Benjamin, A. (2002). *Differentiated instruction: A guide for middle and high school teachers.* Larchmont, NY: Eye on Education.

Black, P., & Wiliam, D. (1998). Assessment and classroom learning. *Assessment in Education, 5*(1), 7–74. Available: http://dx.doi.org/10.1080/0969595980050102

Bransford, J. D., Brown, A. L., & Cocking, R. R. (Eds.). (2000). *How people learn: Brain, mind, experience, and school.* Washington, DC: National Academy Press.

Brookfield, S. D. (1995). *Becoming a critically reflective teacher.* San Francisco: Jossey-Bass.

Bruchac, J. (2001). *Sacajawea.* New York: Scholastic.

Burke, J. (2002). *Tools for thought: Graphic organizers for your classroom.* Portsmouth, NH: Heinemann.

Cain, S. (2012). *Quiet: The power of introverts in a world that can't stop talking.* New York: Broadway Paperbacks.

Choppin, J. (2011). The impact of professional noticing on teachers' adaptations of challenging tasks. *Mathematical Thinking and Learning, 13*(3), 175–197. Available: http://dx.doi.org/10.1080/10986065.2010.495049

Clay, M. M. (2000). *Running records for classroom teachers.* Portsmouth, NH: Heinemann.

Cooper, H., Robinson, J., & Patall, E. A. (2006). Does homework improve academic achievement? A synthesis of research, 1987–2003. *Review of Educational Research, 76*(1), 1–62. Available: http://dx.doi.org/10.3102/0034654 3076001001

Daniels, H. (2001). *Literature circles: Voice and choice in book clubs and reading groups.* York, ME: Stenhouse.

Daniels, H. (2006). What's the next big thing with literature circles? *Voices from the Middle, 13*(4), 10–15.

Dean, C. B., Hubbell, E. R., Pitler, H., & Stone, B. (2012). *Classroom instruction that works: Research-based strategies for increasing student achievement* (2nd ed.). Alexandria, VA: ASCD.

Denenberg, B. (1990). *Stealing home: The story of Jackie Robinson.* New York: Scholastic.

Derry, S. J., & Murphy, D. A. (1986). Designing systems that train learning ability: From theory to practice. *Review of Educational Research, 56,* 1–39. Available: http://dx.doi.org/10.3102/00346543056001001

Dick, W., Carey, L., & Carey, J. O. (2001). *The systematic design of instruction* (5th ed.). New York: Addison Wesley Longman.

Donovan, M. S., & Bransford, J. D. (2005). *How students learn: History, mathematics, and science in the classroom.* Washington, DC: National Research Council.

Duffy, G. G. (2009). *Explaining reading: A resource for teaching concepts, skills, and strategies* (2nd ed.). New York: Guilford.

Dufresne, A., & Kobisagawa, A. (1989). Children's spontaneous allocation of study time: Differential and sufficient aspects. *Journal of Experimental Child Psychology, 47,* 274–296. Available: http://dx.doi.org/10.1016/0022-0965(89)90033-7

Duke, N. K., & Pearson, P. D. (2002). Effective practices for developing reading comprehension. In A. E. Farstup & S. J. Samuels (Eds.), *What research has to say about reading instruction* (3rd ed.) (pp. 205–242). Newark, DE: International Reading Association.

Duke, R. A. (2012). Their own best teachers: How we help and hinder the development of learners' independence. *Music Educators Journal, 99*(2), 36–41. Available: http://dx.doi.org/10.1177/0027432112458956

Dweck, C. S. (2010, October). Even geniuses work hard. *Educational Leadership, 68*(2), 16–20.

Ericsson, K. A., Krampe, R. T., & Tesch-Rober, C. (1993). The role of deliberate practice in the acquisition of expert performance. *Psychological Review, 100*, 363–406.

Fisher, D., & Frey, N. (2007a). *Checking for understanding: Formative assessment techniques for your classroom.* Alexandria, VA: ASCD.

Fisher, D., & Frey, N. (2007b). *Scaffolded writing instruction: Teaching with a gradual-release framework.* New York: Scholastic.

Fisher, D., & Frey, N. (2008). Homework and the gradual release of responsibility: Making "responsibility" possible. *English Journal, 98*(2), 40–45.

Fisher, D., & Frey, N. (2012a). Close reading in elementary schools. *The Reading Teacher, 66*, 179–188.

Fisher, D., & Frey, N. (2012b, February). *Collaborative learning: Ensuring students consolidate understanding* (Engaging the Adolescent Learner). Newark, DE: International Reading Association.

Fisher, D., & Frey, N. (2012c). *Improving adolescent literacy: Content area strategies at work* (3rd ed.). Upper Saddle River, NJ: Pearson.

Fisher, D., & Frey, N. (2012d, September). Making time for feedback. *Educational Leadership, 70*(1), 42–47.

Fisher, D., & Frey, N. (2013). *Common Core English language arts in a PLC at work, grades 3–5.* Bloomington, IN: Solution Tree.

Fisher, D., Frey, N., & Pumpian, I. (2012). *How to create a culture of achievement in your school and classroom.* Alexandria, VA: ASCD.

Flavell, J. H. (1979). Metacognition and cognitive monitoring: A new area of cognitive-developmental inquiry. *American Psychologist, 34*, 906–911. Available: http://dx.doi.org/10.1037/0003-066X.34.10.906

Frank, A. (1953). *The diary of a young girl.* New York: Random House.

Frey, N., & Fisher, D. (2011). *The formative assessment action plan: Practical steps to more successful teaching and learning.* Alexandria, VA: ASCD.

Frey, N., Fisher, D., & Everlove, S. (2009). *Productive group work: How to engage students, build teamwork, and promote understanding.* Alexandria, VA: ASCD.

Frey, N., Fisher, D., & Gonzalez, A. (2010). *Literacy 2.0: Reading and writing in 21st century classrooms.* Bloomington, IN: Solution Tree.

Gallant, R. A. (2000). *Comets, asteroids, and meteorites.* New York: Benchmark Books.

Ganci, C. (2003). *Chief: The life of Peter J. Ganci, a New York City firefighter.* New York: Orchard.

Gladwell, M. (2008). *Outliers: The story of success.* New York: Little, Brown.

Graff, G., & Birkenstein, C. (2009). *They say/I say: The moves that matter in academic writing.* New York: Norton.

Grant, M., Lapp, D., Fisher, D., Johnson, K., & Frey, N. (2012). Purposeful instruction: Mixing up the "I," "we," and "you." *Journal of Adolescent and Adult Literacy, 56*, 45–55. Available: http://dx.doi.org/10.1002/JAAL.00101

Graves, M. F., & Fitzgerald, J. (2003). Scaffolding reading experiences for multilingual classrooms. In G. G. Garcia (Ed.), *English learners: Reaching the highest level of English literacy* (pp. 96–124). Newark, DE: International Reading Association.

Grenier, M., Dyson, B., & Yeaton, P. (2005). Cooperative learning that includes students with disabilities. *Journal of Physical Education, Recreation and Dance, 76*(6), 29–35. Available: http://dx.doi.org/10.1080/07303084.2005.10608264

Guzzetti, B. J., Snyder, T. E., Glass, G. V., & Gamas, W. S. (1993). Promoting conceptual change in science: A comparative meta-analysis of instructional interventions from reading education and science education. *Reading Research Quarterly, 28,* 116–159. Available: http://dx.doi.org/10.2307/747886

Hattie, J., & Timperley, H. (2007). The power of feedback. *Review of Educational Research, 77*(1), 81–112. Available: http://dx.doi.org/10.3102/003465430298487

Hattie, J. A. C. (2009). *Visible learning: A synthesis of over 800 meta-analyses relating to achievement.* New York: Routledge.

Hattie, J. A. C. (2013). Calibration and confidence: Where to next? *Learning and Instruction, 24,* 62–66. Available: http://dx.doi.org/10.1016/j.learninstruc.2012.05.009

Hattie, J. A. C., Brown, G. T., & Keegan, P. (2005). A national teacher-managed, curriculum-based assessment system: Assessment tools for teaching & learning (asTTle). *International Journal of Learning, 10,* 770–778.

Hill, J. D., & Flynn, K. M. (2006). *Classroom instruction that works with English language learners.* Alexandria, VA: ASCD.

Institute for Learning. (n.d.). *Principles of learning.* Retreived from http://ifl.lrdc.pitt.edu/ifl/index.php/resources

International Society for Technology in Education. (2012). *Advancing digital age learning.* Retrieved from http://www.iste.org/standards/nets-for-students

Johnson, D. W., Johnson, R. T., & Smith, K. (1991). *Active learning: Cooperation in the college classroom.* Edina, MN: Interaction Book Company.

Kapur, M. (2008). Productive failure. *Cognition and Instruction, 26,* 379–424. Available: http://dx.doi.org/10.1080/07370000802212669

Kellough, R. D., & Kellough, N. G. (1999). *Secondary school teaching: A guide to methods and resources.* Upper Saddle River, NJ: Prentice Hall.

Kesten, C. (1987). *Independent learning.* Regina, Canada: Saskatchewan Education.

Krull, K. (2003). *Harvesting hope: The story of Cesar Chavez.* San Diego, CA: Harcourt.

Lee, I. (2009). Ten mismatches between teachers' beliefs and written feedback practice. *ELT Journal, 63*(1), 13–22. Available: http://dx.doi.org/10.1093/elt/ccn010

Mason, D. A., & Good, T. L. (1993). Effects of two-group and whole-class teaching on regrouped elementary students' mathematics achievement. *American Educational Research Journal, 30,* 328–360. Available: http://dx.doi.org/10.3102/00028312030002328

McMahon, S. I., Raphael, T. E., Goatley, V. J., & Pardo, L. S. (2007). *The book club connection: Literacy learning and classroom talk.* New York: Teachers College Press.

Michaels, S., O'Connor, C., & Resnick, L. (2008). Deliberative discourse idealized and realized: Accountable talk in the classroom and in civic life. *Studies in*

Philosophy and Education, 27, 283–297. Available: http://dx.doi.org/10.1007/s11217-007-9071-1

Nathan, M. J., & Petrosino, A. (2003). Expert blind spot among preservice teachers. *American Educational Research Journal, 40,* 905–928. Available: http://dx.doi.org/10.3102/00028312040004905

National Association of Colleges and Employers. (2012, June). More than half the class had internship/co-op experience. *Spotlight for Career Services Professionals.* Retrieved from http://www.naceweb.org/s06062012/intern-co-op-experience/?menuID=364&referal=knowledgecenter

National Council of Teachers of Mathematics. (2000). *Principles and standards for school mathematics.* Retrieved from http://standards.nctm.org/document/chapter2/assess.htm

National Governors Association Center for Best Practices, Council of Chief State School Officers. (2010a). *Common Core State Standards for English language arts & literacy in history/social studies, science, and technical subjects.* Washington, DC: Author. Retrieved from http://www.corestandards.org/assets/CCSSI_ELA%20Standards.pdf

National Governors Association Center for Best Practices, Council of Chief State School Officers. (2010b). *Common Core State Standards for mathematics.* Washington, DC: Author. Retrieved from http://www.corestandards.org/assets/CCSSI_Math%20Standards.pdf

Naylor, P. R. (1991). *Shiloh.* New York: Atheneum.

Oczkus, L. D. (2010). *Reciprocal teaching at work: Powerful strategies and lessons for improving reading comprehension* (2nd ed.). Newark, DE: International Reading Association.

Osborne, J., & Dillon, J. (2010). How science works: What is the nature of scientific reasoning and what do we know about students' understanding? In J. Osborne & J. Dillon (Eds.), *Good practice in science teaching: What research has to say* (pp. 20–45). Berkshire, England: McGraw-Hill Education.

Palinscar, A. S., & Brown, A. L. (1984). Reciprocal teaching of comprehension-fostering and comprehension-monitoring activities. *Cognition and Instruction, 1,* 117–175. Available: http://dx.doi.org/10.1207/s1532690xci0102_1

Parker, S. (2005). *Electricity.* New York: DK Publishing.

Partnership for 21st Century Skills. (2009). *Framework for 21st century learning.* Retrieved from http://www.p21.org/overview/skills-framework

Patrick, H., Bangel, N. J., & Jeon, K. (2005). Reconsidering the issue of cooperative learning with gifted students. *Journal for the Education of the Gifted, 29*(1), 90–108.

Pearson, P. D., & Gallagher, G. (1983). The gradual release of responsibility model of instruction. *Contemporary Educational Psychology, 8,* 112–123.

Piaget, J. (1952). *The origins of intelligence in children.* New York: Norton.

Popham, W. J. (2008). *Transformative assessment.* Alexandria, VA: ASCD.

Raphael, T. E., Highfield, K., & Au, K. H. (2006). *QAR now: A powerful and practical framework that develops comprehension and higher-level thinking in all students.* New York: Scholastic.

Resnick, L. (1995). From aptitude to effort: A new foundation for our schools. *Daedalus, 124*(4), 55–62.

Resnick, L. B. (2000). Making America smarter. *Education Week, 18*(40), 38–40.

Rigby. (2004). *Dad* (Rigby PM Collection: PM Starters, No. 1). San Diego, CA: Harcourt.

Ryan, P. M. (2000). *Esperanza rising.* New York: Scholastic.

Singer, S. R., Hilton, M. L., & Schweingruber, H. A. (2006). *America's lab report: Investigations in high school science.* Washington, DC: National Research Council.

Summers, J. J. (2006). Effects of collaborative learning in math on sixth graders' individual goal orientations from a socioconstructivist perspective. *Elementary School Journal, 106,* 273–290.

Tomlinson, C. A., & Imbeau, M. B. (2010). *Leading and managing a differentiated classroom.* Alexandria, VA: ASCD.

U.S. Department of Labor Office of Disability Employment Policy. (2012). *Soft skills to pay the bills—Mastering soft skills for workplace success.* Retrieved from http://www.dol.gov/odep/topics/youth/softskills/#.UMzTF4U_zEg

Vatterott, C. (2009). *Rethinking homework: Best practices that support diverse needs.* Alexandria, VA: ASCD.

Vygotsky, L. S. (1962). *Thought and language.* Cambridge, MA: MIT Press.

Vygotsky, L. S. (1978). *Mind in society.* Cambridge, MA: Harvard University Press.

White, E. B. (1948). Death of a pig. *The Atlantic, 81*(1), 28–33.

Wiggins, G. (1998). *Educative assessment: Designing assessments to inform and improve student performance.* San Francisco: Jossey-Bass.

Wiggins, G., & McTighe, J. (2005). *Understanding by Design* (2nd ed.). Alexandria, VA: ASCD.

Wiliam, D. (2007). Keeping learning on track: Classroom assessment and the regulation of learning. In F. K. Lester Jr. (Ed.), *Second handbook of mathematics teaching and learning* (pp. 1053–1098). Greenwich, CT: Information Age Publishing.

Wilson, J., & Cutting, L. (2001). *Contracts for independent learning: Engaging students in the middle years.* Melbourne: Curriculum Corporation.

Wood, D., Bruner, J. S., & Ross, G. (1976). The role of tutoring and problem solving. *Journal of Child Psychology and Psychiatry, 17,* 89–100. Available: http://dx.doi.org/10.1111/j.1469-7610.1976.tb00381.x

Xu, J., & Wu, H. (2013). Self-regulation of homework behavior: Homework management at the secondary school level. *Journal of Educational Research, 106,* 1–13. Available: http://dx.doi.org/10.1080/00220671.2012.658457

Zhang, J., & Dougherty Stahl, K. A. (2011). Collaborative reasoning: Language-rich discussions for English learners. *The Reading Teacher, 65*(4), 257–260. Available: http://dx.doi.org/10.1002/TRTR.01040

Index

The letter *f* following a page number denotes a figure.

About the Authors

 **Douglas Fisher** is a professor of educational leadership at San Diego State University and a teacher leader at Health Sciences High & Middle College. He is a member of the California Reading Hall of Fame and the recipient of a Celebrate Literacy Award from the International Reading Association, the Farmer Award for Excellence in Writing from the National Council of Teachers of English, and a Christa McAuliffe Award for Excellence in Teacher Education from the American Association of State Colleges and Universities. He has published numerous articles on improving student achievement, and his books include *The Purposeful Classroom: How to Structure Lessons with Learning Goals in Mind; Enhancing RTI: How to Ensure Success with Effective Classroom Instruction and Intervention; Checking for Understanding: Formative Assessment Techniques for Your Classroom; How to Create a Culture of Achievement in Your School and Classroom,* and *Using Data to Focus Instructional Improvement.* He can be reached at dfisher@mail.sdsu.edu.

Nancy Frey is a professor of educational leadership at San Diego State University and a teacher leader at Health Sciences High & Middle College. Before joining the university faculty, Nancy was a special education teacher in the Broward County (Florida) Public Schools, where she taught students at the elementary and middle school levels. She later worked for the Florida Department of Education on a statewide project for supporting students with disabilities in a general education curriculum. Nancy is a recipient of the Christa McAuliffe Award for Excellence in Teacher Education from the American Association of State Colleges and Universities and the Early Career Award from the Literacy Research Association. Her research interests include reading and literacy, assessment, intervention, and curriculum design. She has published many articles and a number of books on literacy and instruction, including *Productive Group Work: How to Engage Students, Build Teamwork, and Promote Understanding; The Formative Assessment Action Plan: Practical Steps to More Successful Teaching and Learning*, and *Guided Instruction: How to Develop Confident and Successful Learners*. She can be reached at nfrey@mail.sdsu.edu.

To learn more about Doug, Nancy, and their work, please visit www.fisherandfrey.com.

Related ASCD Resources: Effective Instruction

At the time of publication, the following ASCD resources were available (ASCD stock numbers appear in parentheses). For up-to-date information about ASCD resources, go to www.ascd.org. You can search the complete archives of *Educational Leadership* at http://www.ascd.org/el.

ASCD EDge Group

Exchange ideas and connect with other educators interested in effective classroom instruction on the social networking site ASCD EDge™ at http://ascdedge.ascd.org/

Print Products

The Art and Science of Teaching: A Comprehensive Framework for Effective Instruction by Robert J. Marzano (#107001)

Checking for Understanding: Formative Assessment Techniques for Your Classroom by Douglas Fisher and Nancy Frey (#107023)

Guided Instruction: How to Develop Confident and Successful Learners by Nancy Frey and Douglas Fisher (#111017)

Learning for Keeps: Teaching the Strategies Essential for Creating Independent Learners by Rhoda Koenig (#111003)

Productive Group Work: How to Engage Students, Build Teamwork, and Promote Understanding by Nancy Frey, Douglas Fisher, and Sandi Everlove (#109018)

Enhancing Professional Practice: A Framework for Teaching, 2nd Edition by Charlotte F. Danielson (#106034)

Video

The Art and Science of Teaching 2 DVD Series (#608074); also available as a digital download

Never Work Harder Than Your Students: The Journey to Great Teaching (#610009)

Problem-Based Learning for the 21st Century Classroom 2 DVD Series (#610014)

For more information: send e-mail to member@ascd.org; call 1-800-933-2723 or 703-578-9600, press 2; send a fax to 703-575-5400; or write to Information Services, ASCD, 1703 N. Beauregard St., Alexandria, VA 22311-1714 USA.